First Edition 2021

ISBN 978 1 8380086 9 7

The information in this book is
knowledge. All recommendatio.
part of the Publisher, who also d                                    ..ıon
with the use of specific details or                        .ɔ ɒook.

**British Library Cataloguing-in-Publication Data**
A catalogue record for this book is available from the British Library.

Published by Destinworld Publishing Ltd.
**www.destinworld.com**

Cover design by Ken Leeder
Cover image Copyright © Glen Moray Distillery
Maps by Simonetta Giori

2  *Still at Annandale distillery*

# CONTENTS

*Casks at Benromach Distillery*

# Introduction

SCOTLAND AND WHISKY go together very well. Chances are it comes to mind when you think of the country, alongside kilts, bagpipes and the Loch Ness Monster. But we are not here to belittle or simplify the *water of life* which first emerged at Lindores Abbey in Fife around 1494, nor are we here to turn this important industry into a theme park-like attraction here purely for entertainment.

Whisky production in Scotland is big business and an important part of the country's identity. It is a major employer and brings in much revenue each year with its global reach and widespread appeal. It has naturally had its ups and downs as interest faded, supplies dwindled, and world wars and prohibition stifled demand. Yet today, the interest in and demand for Scottish whisky is at an all-time high and the range of tastes and styles is phenomenal.

This book hopes to be your guide to Scotland's whisky distilleries. We've tried to include every single one, from the smallest to the largest and the newest to the oldest. The growth of the industry and accessibility to newcomers means, however, that there are exciting new distilleries popping up all the time around the country. There are some included here that are only a few years old and still waiting for their products to mature. A single malt needs to age for a minimum of three years to qualify, and many connoisseurs prefer something that has aged longer, and so these are very much distilleries to keep an eye on in the future.

Most traditional whisky distilleries in Scotland can date their founding back well over a hundred and fifty years, with the oldest still in operation today, Glenturret, dating from 1775 (although the closed Littlemill distillery of 1772 still exists). These often started in farms as a side business to bring in extra income, usually without a license. As the industry changed, many of these illicit distilleries became legal and grew, and their buildings still survive in many cases.

Yet over the centuries many new distilleries have sprung up, sometimes created on an industrial scale with less than attractive buildings never meant to be anything other than whisky-producing machines.

The idea of visiting distilleries came along much more recently. These places of industry and business were not designed to welcome the public, and often posed hazardous with all the machinery, noise and tumbledown old buildings. However, the rise in tourism to Scotland and the popularity of its whisky naturally attracted visitors to come and see how it was produced, and distilleries quickly learnt how this could become in an important extra revenue stream. Soon many distilleries were offering tours, tastings as well as shops to sell their bottles and cafes serving refreshments. It is now a huge part of Scotland's tourism appeal and has only grown with the revival of the popularity of single malt whisky.

With each distillery listed here we have tried to indicate where visitor facilities exist, along with opening days and times, details of tours, and where to find more information. During the Covid-19 pandemic all of Scotland's distilleries were forced to close their doors to visitors. As they reopen there is a good chance that details may have changed, or that some may not offer the same experiences as before. We are grateful to the distilleries for giving us as much up-to-date information as possible at the time of going to print, but please make sure you contact the distillery or check their website in advance of visiting to be sure they are open.

There are also more to come, with new independent distilleries opening and creating their own whiskies (often starting with gin while the whisky matures). Some older distilleries are also being reopened, with both Port Ellen on Islay and Brora near Clynelish currently being restored by owners Diageo to begin producing again using original equipment and buildings.

Whether you're a whisky connoisseur or a casual visitor to Scotland, we hope this book encourages you to visit some of the distilleries which are found all around the country. Their staff are knowledgeable and passionate about what they produce, and by visiting you can get to know their history and sample their craft straight from the cask.

**Matt Falcus**
**Editor**

# How Whisky is Made

**IF YOU'RE NEW** to whisky, or travelling around Scotland discovering the different distilleries and their products, you may be wondering how this fine and popular spirit is made. You may also wonder how the flavours can differ so much from one distillery or region to the next, and how that is achieved.

The secret of making whisky has existed for centuries, possibly longer, and it's remarkably simple. However, perfecting it is a continuing process for each distiller involved in its creation, and that's how we are repeatedly offered new bottlings and tastes year after year. In fact, it is amazing that creating so many different flavours and styles from so few ingredients and a largely formulaic process is possible.

# The Ingredients

The ingredients used in producing whisky are: grain, water and yeast. It's really that simple.

**GRAIN IN ITSELF** comes in many different types, and should not be confused with the term 'grain whisky' which usually refers to whisky produced with corn or wheat. There are many types of grain that can be used, including barley, corn, wheat and rye. Barley is by far the most common used in Scottish whisky.

In Scotland, barley is grown widely and, as you would expect, water sources are widespread. These each filter through different types of ground and vegetation, often over a long period. This is often where individual distilleries gain their own unique flavours, thanks to the qualities within the water used to produce their whisky.

# The Process

**BEGINNING WITH THE** barley as a basic ingredient, it is first of all malted. This involves moistening the barley with water so that germination begins and an enzyme is given out which converts its starches into sugar. It is then left to dry on large floors, which halts the germination process. Some distilleries malt their own barley, often burning peat during the drying process to add a smoky flavour. Others import barley that has already been imported.

The next stage sees the malted barley added to a large mash tun and mixed with hot water. This serves the purpose of extracting the sugars, and creates a porridge-like substance known as wort or mash. The sugary water mixture by product is then extracted from the grist and added to a washback where yeast is mixed in and heated up.

This process, known as fermentation, can take at least two days, if not three or four, depending on the distillery's process and ingredients. The result is a mildly alcoholic liquid known as wash, which is then distilled.

Distillation is completed in large conical vats known as stills, and these vary from one distillery to the next in terms of size and shape. You will often see the stills on a tour of a distillery. First, the wash is boiled, leaving the alcohol to vaporize off first and flow into the shell-and-tube condenser, where it is cooled and condensed back into a liquid known as spirit. Sometimes distilleries use a worm tub instead of the condenser, which creates a heavier spirit. Before the next stage, in Scotch whisky production the spirit is usually distilled a second time in a spirit still.

The usable part of the spirit from the second distillation is sent to the spirit safe, where distillers can sample it to get a flavour of how the batch (or indeed a brand new whisky) might ultimately taste.

The rest it sent to fill barrels, where the maturation process takes place. Distilleries place a lot of importance on the barrels they use. These are usually American oak barrels, which have been used in bourbon production, or sherry casks used in the production of Spanish sherry. Scotch whisky is always filled into these used casks as the flavours are important to the final taste of the product.

To be legally called a Scottish single malt whisky, the produce needs to have matured for a minimum of three years. Typically, the longer the time spent in barrels in the right storage conditions, the more the whisky's flavour will mature and its flavour become more complex, hence older bottlings commanding a much higher purchase price.

Once the whisky has matured in its barrels for the prescribed amount of time, bottling and distribution takes place. In the case of blended whiskies, the produce is sent off to a specialist blender to combine with other malts and bottle.

# SCOTLAND'S
## Whisky Regions

ORKNEY
• Kirkwall

HOY

• Thurso

• Wick

*Moray Firth*

• Stornoway

LEWIS

• Lochinver

• Brora

*The Minch*

NORTH UIST

• Ullapool

• Tain

• Invergordon

SPEYSIDE

• Nairn
• Dingwall
• Torridon
• Inverness
Forres •
• Elgin
• Keith
Banff •
Fraserbur
Macduff •

Craigellachie •
• Dufftown
• Huntly
• Oldmeldr
• Inverurie

SOUTH UIST

• Portree

SKYE

• Kyle of Lochalsh

• Fort Augustus

Grantownon-Spey

• Aviemore

• Kingussie

• Ballater

• Aberdeen
• Banchory

*Sea of the Hebrides*

• Mallaig

• Fort William

HIGHLANDS

• Stonehaven

• Glencoe

• Pitlochry

• Aberfeldy

• Blairgowrie

• Montrose

• Tobermory

MULL

• Oban

• Dundee

• Arbroath
• Carnoustie

• Inveraray
• Crieff
• Perth

• Callander
• Auchterarder

• St. Andrews

JURA

• Stirling
• Kinross
• Glenrothes

ISLAY

• Lochgilphead

• Dumbarton

• North Berwick

Port Askaig •

• Greenock

• Glasgow

EDINBURGH

ISLAY

• Tarbert

• Kilmarnock

• Melrose
• Coldstre

Port Ellen •

ARRAN

• Troon
• Ayr

LOWLANDS

• Hawick

• Campbeltown

• Moffat

## CAMPBELTOWN

• Dumfries
• Annan

• Wigtown
• Castle Douglas

• Stranraer

*North Channel*

# Scotland's Whisky Regions

*"The water source of Arran distillery"*

**Whisky is produced** all across Scotland, from the borders to the remote islands. However, the country is divided into five (some say six) whisky-producing regions and you will often see this written on the label of single malt bottles.

The regions are: Campbeltown, Highland, Islay, Lowland and Speyside. Some say Islands – that is, the Hebrides, Orkneys, Mull, Skye, Jura and Arran – is a separate region. But in this book, and in many other guides, distilleries in these places are included in the Highland region.

*"Scapa is one of two distilleries in the rugged landscape of the Orkney Islands"*

Each whisky producing region has its own styles, strengths and flavours which often characterize the whiskies produced there. Lowland whiskies are usually light, smooth, soft and gentle. Speyside whiskies have a mix of peat, fruit and spice, and are often matured in sherry casks. Islay is famous for its peaty and smoky flavours, like the medicinal Laphroaig or Lagavulin. Campbeltown whiskies tell of the sea, with salty, robust flavours. And Highland, covering the largest area, has a mix of all styles from light and smooth to salty and peaty.

*"The sprawling site of Tomatin's distillery"*

There is no right or wrong place to start your whisky journey, unless taking in different whiskies in a single sitting, where a smoky and peaty Islay might overpower a smooth Lowland. Each region has highly regarded distilleries and whiskies which suit different pallets and work with different food pairings. The key is to discover the flavours that work for you.

Each region has its own history of whisky producing, too. By visiting the distilleries in this book you'll learn of the stories from each. Speyside has become the densest whisky-producing region in the world, whilst Campbeltown has lost much of its industry that once thrived, and Lowland is seeing a growth in new and boutique distilleries popping up, with a push towards organic and sustainable production.

*"Ncn'ean is one of a number of new distilleries focusing on organic and sustainable whisky production"*

*Springbank*

# CAMPBELTOWN
## Whisky Region

ARRAN

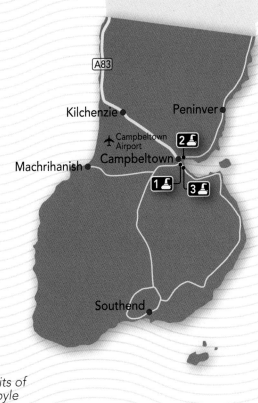

A83

Kilchenzie

Peninver

Campbeltown Airport

2

Campbeltown

Machrihanish

1

3

Southend

Straits of
Moyle

1.   GLENGYLE
2.   GLEN SCOTIA
3.   SPRINGBANK

# Glengyle

Glengyle was founded in Campbeltown in 1872 by William Mitchell and, like many of the town's distilleries, was closed down in 1925. The chairman of Springbank, one of only two remaining Campbeltown distilleries, eventually bought the historic Glengyle site in the early 2000s, re-opening it in 2004, reviving it and, importantly, helping to keep the Campbeltown whisky-producing region active since so few distilleries previously remained.

Interestingly, since the Glengyle name was already in use by Loch Lomond, the revived distillery named its new whisky range Kilkerran. Glengyle distillery is a combination of old and new but quite different to Springbank. Most of the production happens in one large open plan space, between October and December each year, using Springbank staff. There is a stainless steel lauter mash tun but wooden wash backs are still employed. With experimentation key to their produce, Glengyle make unpeated, super heavily peated, triple distilled and a core lightly peated, double distilled spirit. They have an annual production of around 92,000 litres.

With it being so new, a range of 'Work In Progress' whiskies is released every six months or so. These have become popular. The two core expressions in the range are a 12-Year-Old and a 16-Year-Old.

**Address:** 9 Bolgam Street, Campbeltown, PA28 6HZ
**Phone:** +44 1586 552009
**Web:** www.kilkerran.scot

## Visitor Centre

Tours are operated on a seasonal basis, and in conjunction with the Springbank distillery nearby. They run Monday to Friday Between November and April, with more during the summer months. Tickets can be booked online or in person, and must be collected from the Springbank distillery (see separate entry).

# Glen Scotia

One of Campbeltown's few distilleries, Glen Scotia was founded in 1832 and has a strong history at the heart of this small whisky producing region. With its malt prized by American blenders because of its strong taste, it was forced to halt production during the Prohibition era. It closed again during the 1980s, but has since re-opened and, under new ownership, is going strong once again. Glen Scotia produces a range of core and limited releases. It still has the original design in its buildings and, with a limited staff, has an output of around 600,000 litres per year using one wash and one spirit still. Its water source is Crosshill Loch.

A visitor centre and shop take you through the history of this place, and it takes an important part in the Campbeltown Malts Festival. Its dinners and dunnage tastings always sell out, and recently this has gone 'global' with virtual tastings and tours (see www.glentscotia.com/festival/)

**Address:** 12 High St, Campbeltown PA28 6DS
**Phone:** +44 1586 552288
**Web:** www.glenscotia.com

## Visitor Centre

Distillery tours lasting an hour are run a few times per day, or you can enjoy one of a variety of tasting tours lasting up to 90 minutes, giving the opportunity to try the core and limited edition Glen Scotia malts. The distillery is open Monday to Saturday and booking is advised.

# Springbank

Springbank has the distinction of being the oldest independent family owned distillery in Scotland. It was established by Archibald Mitchell in 1828 on the site of a still he ran illicitly prior to making things official and legal. A fifth generation of the family, Hedley Mitchell, is in charge today.

Of particular note here is that Springbank completes the entire process of producing its whisky on site, from malting to bottling, including all maturation. In fact, given its age and unusual history, it is often thought of as a 'working museum' and draws fans of whisky production from all over the world. The wash still is heated by both direct fire and steam coils and the cast iron open-topped mash tun is Victorian in age. These are just two of the more unusual features you can see when visiting.

The distillery uses three stills which allow the production process to be adapted to create different styles of spirit. Their main Springbank range is complemented by a more heavily peated range called Longrow (first produced in 1973) and an unpeated range called Hazelburn (first produced in 1997).

In the early 2000s Sprinbank acquired the disused Glengyle site and resurrected it (see separate entry), sharing staff between the two, and today run tours in conjunction with both distilleries.

**Address:** 9 Bolgam Street, Campbeltown, Argyll, PA28 6HZ
**Phone:** +44 1586 552009
**Web:** www.springbank.scot
**Social Media:**
@springbank1828v

## Visitor Centre

Journey through this historic Campeltown distillery with its unique setup on a tour to discover the process. These can be booked online, and tours of the associated Glengyle distillery can also be booked. You can also book on an annual 5-day Whisky School where you'll learn the process in more detail and see the results.

*Aberfeldy*

# HIGHLAND
## Whisky Region

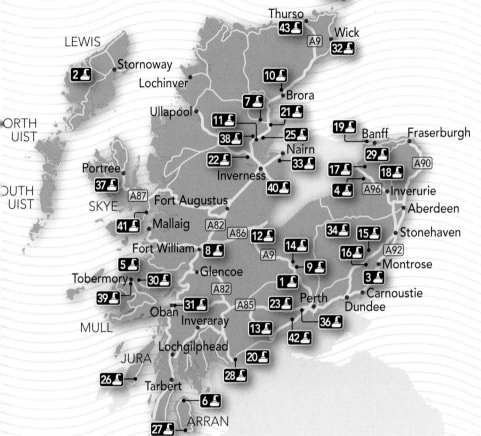

| | | | | | |
|---|---|---|---|---|---|
| 1. | ABERFELDY | 16. | GLENCADAM | 31. | OBAN |
| 2. | ABHAINN DEARG | 17. | GLENDRONACH, THE | 32. | PULTENEY |
| 3. | ARBIKIE | 18. | GLEN GARIOCH | 33. | ROYAL BRACKLA |
| 4. | ARDMORE | 19. | GLENGLASSAUGH | 34. | ROYAL LOCHNAGAR |
| 5. | ARDNAMURCHAN | 20. | GLENGOYNE | 35. | SCAPA |
| 6. | ISLE OF ARRAN | 21. | GLENMORANGIE | 36. | STRATHEARN |
| 7. | BALBLAIR | 22. | GLEN ORD | 37. | TALISKER |
| 8. | BEN NEVIS | 23. | GLENTURRET | 38. | TEANINICH |
| 9. | BLAIR ATHOL | 24. | HIGHLAND PARK | 39. | TOBERMORY |
| 10. | CLYNELISH | 25. | INVERGORDON | 40. | TOMATIN |
| 11. | DALMORE | 26. | ISLE OF JURA | 41. | TORABHAIG |
| 12. | DALWHINNIE | 27. | LAGG | 42. | TULLIBARDINE |
| 13. | DEANSTON | 28. | LOCH LOMOND | 43. | WOLFBURN |
| 14. | EDRADOUR | 29. | MACDUFF | | |
| 15. | FETTERCAIRN | 30. | NCN'EAN | | |

# Aberfeldy

Lovers of whisky may usually turn their noses up at blends, preferring the quality and flavours of a well-crafted single malt. Yet as you read through this book you will no doubt notice just how many distilleries today make a living off providing malt for blends, and have always done so. In fact, blends are often the most commercial types of whisky, selling more bottles than any other, and are the entry point for new whisky fans the world over. True whisky connoisseurs will, therefore, appreciate the value of blends and the important part they play in Scottish whisky production.

And so we arrive at Aberfeldy. A Highland distillery in Perthshire, it is home to one of the biggest

**Address:** Aberfeldy, Perthshire PH15 2EB
**Phone:** +44 1887 822010
**Web:** www.dewarsaberfeldydistillery.com

## Visitor Centre

Voted one of Scotland's best visitor attractions, Dewar's Aberfeldy Whisky Distillery has a large visitor centre which displays the history of whisky production (with an emphasis on blending). It also has a café, restaurant, bar and shop. A range of guided tours of the distillery are available, with tastings. Booking is advised.

whisky visitor centres in Scotland, and this is built around the part this distillery has played in blends. Aberfeldy dates to 1898 and was created by John Dewar & Sons. Thomas Dewar was instrumental in the art of crafting blended whisky here, and so this distillery has always survived on creating malts for blends, particularly Dewars.

Of course, Aberfeldy also produces a range of award-winning single malts in the 12-, 18- and 21-year-old ranges. It also recently released a 40-year-old single cask edition which has rested in three separate American oak casks since 1978. Today it is owned by Bacardi and has four stills in use – two wash and two spirit – producing up to 3.5 million litres per year. Its water source is Pitilie Burn, a tributary of the River Tay. Its buildings feature that familiar pagoda top on the maltings, and today many visitors come here to learn about whisky production.

# Abhainn Dearg

Founded in 2008, Abhainn Dearg is a fairly new craft whisky distillery on the Isle of Lewis. This is the only distillery in the Outer Hebrides, and the first legal one since the 1850s. It is also the most remote Scottish whisky distillery. Now able to release something of age, its first 10-year-old bottlings are available.

In case you were wondering, it's pronounced *Aveen Jarræk*, which means Red River.

**Visitor Centre**

Distillery tours are available Monday to Friday (and Saturday in the summer) on the hour from 11am to 4pm (except 1pm). Try to arrive in plenty of time.

**Address:** Carnish, Isle of Lewis HS2 9EX
**Phone:** +44 1851 672429
**Web:** www.abhainndeargdistillery.co.uk

# Arbikie Highland Estate Distillery

A modern, experimental, Highland style distillery which also produces gin, vodka and cocktails. Its whiskies are created from locally-grown barley and rye and the distillery's own underground lagoon of filtered rainwater. But you'll have to wait a little longer, as its produce is still maturing, with plans to release 14-, 18- and 21-year-old bottlings. That takes it to the late 2020s. However, 2015 first-release casks are available to purchase. Flavours will be salty, rich and honeyed, from the use of both bourbon and sherry casks.

**Visitor Centre**

No

**Address:** Inverkeilor, Arbroath DD11 4UZ
**Phone:** +44 1241 830770
**Web:** www.arbikie.com

# The Ardmore

Occupying a lofty spot on the Aberdeen-to-Inverness railway line (which helped with distribution), The Ardmore produces blends for Teacher's Highland Cream, and also producing its own 12-year-old single malt and some exclusive bottles. For a Speyside distillery it has a notably peatiness. It has eight stills in operation, producing up to 5.4 million litres per annum.

**Visitor Centre**

No

**Address:** Kennethmont, Aberdeenshire AB54 4NH
**Phone:** +44 1464 831213
**Web:** www.ardmorewhisky.com

Isle of Arran

# Isle of Arran

One of the most incredible locations of all Scottish distilleries, Isle of Arran at Lochranza is also one of the more recent. It was established in 1993 on a location across the water from Robert Burns' birthplace

**Address:** Lochranza Distillery, Lochranza, Isle of Arran KA27 8HJ
**Phone:** +44 1770 830264
**Web:** www.arranwhisky.com

## Visitor Centre

Visitors are able to book in advance for tours to learn more about the distillery. Isle of Arran also has a cafe known as CASKS which sells refreshments and local produce, as well as the whiskies produced here.

at Alloway, and has grown into one of the best-known names in Scottish whisky. This was the first distillery to open on Arran for 150 years (joined more recently by Lagg).

The first whisky to emerge from this distillery was The Arran Malt 10-year-old in 2006. It was followed up by a 12-year-old in 2008 and 18-year-old in 2015, and there have been various limited

editions since.

Arran's whiskies are produced using water from the nearby Lochna Davie above the distillery, forming part of the unique, warm conditions which aid the production of the spirit on Arran. The success of this modest distillery, which opened with four washbacks and a pair of stills, has meant expansion to cater for an ambitious future.

# Ardnamurchan

Proud to be Scotland's greenest distillery, Arnamurchan (owned by Adelphi) is built around sustainability through hydro-electric power and woodchip boilers, and reuse of draff and by products as fertiliser and animal feed. This is a scenic distillery in a remote part of

western Scotland, and it builds on a heritage of distilling in the area dating back to 1826.

Officially opened by HRH The Princess Royal on 25th July 2014, Ardnamurchan is in the process of maturing its first produce, with the aim of releasing its single malt in 2021. It has two stills and seven washbacks in use and sources its water from springs rising behind the distillery, as well as the Glenmore River.

**Address:** Glenbeg, Ardnamurchan PH36 4JG
**Phone:** +44 1972 500285
**Web:** www.adelphidistillery.com

## Visitor Centre

Standard, Premium and Connoisseur's and Manager's tours are available, each with a different level of depth and tasting. The visitor centre includes a bar and shop. Open Daily.

# Balblair

Set in a scenic part of the Highlands, alongside Dornoch Firth, Balblair is an old distillery. It was opened in 1790 and struggled in its early years as illegal distillers nearby undercut owner John Ross, who was dutifully paying taxes on what he produced. It closed for a while between 1911 and 1948 and is now owned by Inver House Distillery. Using time-intensive methods, Balblair produces flavour-intensive malts, describing their work as "a craft, not a process." There are only one wash and one spirit still in use here. Traditionally Balblair would release whiskies marked with the year in which they were distilled, known as a vintage, but today produces a core range of aged single malts in unusual-shaped bottles.

**Address:** Edderton, Tain IV19 1LB
**Phone:** +44 1862 821273
**Web:** www.balblair.com

## Visitor Centre

The Time Capsule room tells the story of Balblair, with sights and sounds to enhance the experience. There's also a shop, and you can take a tour of the distillery and even bottle your own. Open Monday to Friday. Booking is advised.

# Blair Athol

Established as the Aldour Distillery – named after the Allt Dour water source, running from the nearby Grampian mountains – in 1798, this distillery soon foundered. It was resurrected in 1826 as Blair Athol. It gradually grew until US prohibition and the Second World War hit in the 1930s, but was saved and rebuilt in 1949. Today it produces whisky for Bell's blends. A few single malt bottlings have also been produced.

**Address:** Perth Rd, Pitlochry PH16 5LY
**Phone:** +44 1796 482003
**Web:** www.malts.com/en-gb/distilleries/blair-athol

## Visitor Centre

A popular attraction in Pitlochry. Blair Athol has a visitor centre open daily from 10am, with gift shop and various tours, tastings and master classes. Must be booked in advance.

# Ben Nevis

Even Japanese whisky takes a strong influence from that produced in Scotland, and Ben Nevis distillery in Fort William is responsible for sending malt around the world to produce the popular Black Nikka blend. In fact, Asahi Breweries, which produces Nikka, owns Ben Nevis. For this reason the visitor centre here is popular with visiting Japanese tourists.

But the history of Ben Nevis goes much farther back. Built in 1825 as one of the earliest licenced distilleries, it produced the popular Long John blend for many years (named after the distillery's founder "Long John" MacDonald).

A range of core single malts are also produced under the Ben Nevis name, as well as independent and cask bottlings.

**Address:** Lochy Bridge, Fort William PH33 6TJ
**Phone:** +44 1397 702476
**Web:** www.bennevisdistillery.com

## Visitor Centre

The Ben Nevis visitor centre opened in 1991 and is open Monday to Friday (plus weekends in the summer). It is located in the former bottling hall, and mascot Hector McDram will reveal the Legend of the Dew of Ben Nevis in a fun audio visual presentation. You can also tour the distillery, eat in the restaurant and buy a bottle.

# Clynelish

Clynelish is a distillery site dating back to 1819. The current buildings were constructed in 1967 to cope with growing production, while the original distillery was kept on under the Brora name until being mothballed in 1983. Brora is one of the world's rarest whiskies to own. The buildings are currently being brought back into life.

Much of Clynelish's work was in producing peaty malts for blends, and is most commonly used today in Johnnie Walker Gold Label Reserve. It does, however, produce some single malt bottlings.

The distillery has six stills, uses both sherry and bourbon casks, and produces up to 4.8 million litres per annum. It is a popular visitor attraction.

**Address:** Clynelish Distillery, Brora Sutherland, KW9 6LR
**Phone:** +44 1408 623000
**Web:** www.malts.com/en-row/distilleries/clynelish

## Visitor Centre

A popular visitor centre attraction, as well as tours of the distillery, were on offer before Covid. Currently a major tourist investment project is underway which will see Clynelish re-open bigger and better in the future.

# Dalmore

The location of The Dalmore's distillery was carefully chosen, with plentiful availability of good quality barley from the Black Isle peninsula across the Cromarty Firth, water from the River Alness, and local supplies of peat. It was founded in 1839 by Alexander Matheson, and sold to the Mackenzie family in 1891, with whom it grew over the next century.

Today Whyte & Mackay are the operators of the distillery, with whisky produced by The Dalmore as one of the main components to its namesake blend.

But The Dalmore also produces its own single malts. For years its 12-year-old was the only bottling, but this has now grown to include other ages, limited editions, and even the 1263 King Alexander III which commemorates the year the Mackenzie clan saved the king from a wild stag. This event is also borne out by the inclusion of a stag's head on all of its product bottles today.

**Address:** Dalmore, Alness IV17 0UT
**Phone:** +44 1349 882362
**Web:** www.thedalmore.com

## Visitor Centre

Tours of the distillery which give an insight into their history and crafting process are available Monday to Friday (and Saturdays in summer), but must be booked in advance.

The Dalmore's distillery is fairly functional in design, with traditional buildings. It incorporates four flat-top wash stills, four spirit stills with water coolers, and has a capacity of 4.2 million litres per year. Maturation is accomplished in two different kinds of casks – American oak, and hand-selected sherry casks.

As an example of a distillery which has successfully transitioned from merely providing malts for blends to creating its own single-malt product range, various rare bottles have sold for in excess of £100,000 in auction, and one collection of 12 bottles achieved £987,500.

# Dalwhinnie

Dalwhinnie might seem like an unlikely place for a distillery and major tourist attraction, but it is both of those. Built high up in the Cairngorms National Park, it was for a long time Scotland's highest distillery at over 1,000ft above sea level. It is also Scotland's coldest distillery, going by local average temperatures. Even though it is quite well situated just off the A9, and has its own railway station, it can still be difficult to get there in winter. Its meeting point between two ancient roads inspires its name – Dalwhinnie mean "plain of meetings" in Gaelic.

This distillery started life in 1898. It was bought by an American company in 1905, and today is owned by Diageo. The distillery was rebuilt just before World War II following a fire, but then went into hibernation during the war.

While it mostly produces whisky for blends like Black & White, Dalwhinnie also produces a 15-year-old Highland single malt and various limited edition bottlings.

A visitor centre opened in 1991 and it is one of the largest and most popular in a distillery in Scotland, drawing many tourists each year.

**Address:** General Wade's Military Road, Dalwhinnie, Inverness-shire PH19 1AB
**Phone:** +44 1540 672219
**Web:** www.malts.com/en-row/distilleries/dalwhinnie

## Visitor Centre

Dalwhinnie has a large visitor centre with shop and plenty of tours and tastings. These include tours of the distillery, masterclasses and even the chance to taste some of the rarer bottlings. Must be booked in advance. Open daily from 10am.

# Deanston

Deanston is an example of a distillery which has repurposed buildings to create a whisky-making enterprise. Set in a former cotton mill dating from the 1780s on the banks of the River Teith in the village of Deanston (a few miles outside of Stirling), it was turned into a distillery in 1965.

The first single malt produced was Old Bannockburn, alongside the Teith Mill blend. Today Deanston 12-year-old is the main single malt. It is produced in one of Scotland's largest open-topped mash tuns, and pot stills which have upward sloping lyne arms and boiling balls. Water from the River Teith is used to produce the whisky, and also to power the distillery, which is completely self-sufficient for its power needs. It was also Scotland's first distillery to produce organic whisky, and shuns the modern computerised methods used, preferring to use traditional techniques. This seems to fit the surroundings of this old mill.

Easily reached from Glasgow, Stirling, or as part of a visit to Loch Lomond & the Trossachs National Park, Deanston offers tours, tastings and a café.

**Address:** Teith Rd, Deanston, Doune FK16 6AG
**Phone:** +44 1786 843010
**Web:** www.deanstonmalt.com

## Visitor Centre

The shop and café are open every day inside the mill's former canteen room. Tours offering a guided visit to the distillery, as well as tastings are on offer and should be booked via their website.

# Edradour

Edradour is the little distillery that had big plans. Essentially a traditional farm distillery, established in 1825, it has never really grown despite coming under the ownership of Pernod Richard from 1975. Today it is owned by the Signatory Vintage Scotch Whisky Company, who have built a second plant over the river to expand production.

The main produce of Edradour is a range of independent single malts including peated and cask strength varieties.

It is worth visiting this little distillery in a picturesque part of Scotland just to see how traditional methods and an independent spirit can bring a unique outlook to whisky production, and some really interesting tastes.

**Address:** Pitlochry PH16 5JP
**Phone:** +44 1796 472095
**Web:** www.edradour.com

## Visitor Centre

Open Monday to Saturday in summer and Monday to Friday in winter from 10am. On offer are 1.5 hour guided tours, whisky tastings or more in-depth events. There's a gift shop to buy a bottle in, too.

# Fettercairn

Fettercairn means "true" in the local Gaelic language, and this small distillery has been a part of this landscape since the 1820s. Originally sited further north on a farm, when it was bought by Sir Alexander Ramsay and turned into a larger scale facility he moved it to the village location where you'll find it today. Today it's part of Whyte & Mackay's empire, but still welcomes visitors to learn about its heritage and sample its produce.

**Visitor Centre**

A 45-minite tour the distillery, where you'll learn about its history and how their whiskies are made, and enjoy a dram in the shop at the end. Bookable through their website, or by turning up.

**Address:** Distillery Road, Fettercairn, Laurencekirk AB30 1YB
**Phone:** +44 141 248 5771
**Web:** www.fettercairnwhisky.com

# Glencadam

Founded in 1825, two years after distilling was legalised, Glencadam is named after the 'Tenements of Caldhame', or plots of land in Brechin given for food production, situated in the area around the distillery. Glencadam has undergone various changes of ownership, and was even closed down for various periods. Its mature whisky has been traditionally used in blending, but it also has a nice range of its own bottlings, both regular and limited editions, and many have won awards.

Being the only remaining distillery in Angus, Glencadam has exclusive rights to water springs at The Moorans, almost 9 miles away, as well as nearby Barry Burn. Its pure flavour is a result of not using peated barley. It still uses two stills, like the day it was founded.

## Visitor Centre

By appointment only.

**Address:** Brechin, Angus, DD9 7PA
**Phone:** +44 1356 622217
**Web:** www.glencadamwhisky.com

# The Glendronach

Of 1826 vintage, Glendronach has passed through many hands in the intervening years. It was one of the sources of Teacher's blend. Today it produces its own single malts, sourced from the Dronac burn which flows by the distillery and gives it its name. It is a very scenic location and its buildings, now listed, are historic and traditional.

Thanks to the use of sherry casks, its whiskies have a sweet caramel richness to their flavour.

## Visitor Centre

Daily tours are offered from 10am to 4pm taking in the distillery and offering a tasting of some of the produce.

**Address:** Forgue By Huntly, Aberdeenshire, AB54 6DB
**Phone:** +44 131 456 2679
**Web:** www.glendronachdistillery.com

# Glen Garioch

One of Scotland's earliest distilleries, Glan Garioch was founded in 1797 and is still going strong.

Much of its life was spent producing for blenders, which kept it in favour thanks to its popular flavour and quality. Its water source is the enigmatic Silent Spring, which is neither seen nor heard, but presumably of very good quality.

If you're visiting Glen Garioch take care to pronounce the name propertly. Garioch is actually *Geery*, in local dialect. It is the name of the fertile land on which it sits in this part of Aberdeenshire. It uses the fine barley of nearby Oldmeldrum, which adds to the quality.

With four stills, Glen Garioch is now owned by Morrison Bowmore Distillers and continues to produce for blends, alongside a core range of single malts which have won many awards.

## Visitor Centre

The historic Glen Garioch distillery has a visitor centre and gift shop in its former maltings. Tours are available year-round Mondays to Saturdays, with booking advisable.

**Address:** Distillery Road, Oldmeldrum, Inverurie, Aberdeenshire AB51 0ES
**Phone:** +44 1651 873450
**Web:** www.glengarioch.com

# Glenglassaugh

Glenglassaugh is set in a beautiful location and still uses traditional methods in creating its whisky. IT uses the Glassaugh Springs as a water source and nearby farms for barley. It opened in 1875, buoyed on by the excellent produce of illicit distillers in the area.

The distillery has changed hands many times over the years. For a long period it was mothballed, reopening in 2008 under the new ownership of Brown-Forman. Its buildings date from the 1960s, so are not particularly attractive compared to its surroundings.

As well as producing whisky for some famous blends, Glenglassaugh is also producing award winning single malts of its own. Its core range is topped by a 51-year-old bottling, and its 40-year-old has won best in class in the past. It also produces limited editions.

Glenglassaugh has a fairly modest 1 million litres per annum output.

**Address:** Portsoy, Banff AB45 2SQ
**Phone:** +44 131 335 5135
**Web:** www.glenglassaugh.com

## Visitor Centre

A visit to Glenglassaugh is a chance to experience and learn about the traditional methods still used at this distillery. It's also a very scenic place to visit, even if the buildings are less so. Open year-round Monday to Friday (and weekends from May to September). Pay a little extra for tastings.

# Glengoyne

If you're a fan of the splendour of the Scottish countryside and the scenery it can often reveal, then a visit to Glengoyne is a must. Surely one of the most attractive locations of any distillery in Scotland, this site in Stirlingshire even has its own waterfall to see. Nearby are also reed beds where spent yeast is filtered, and eventually the water re-enters the water system in a very environmentally-friendly way.

Glengoyne, founded as the Burnfoot Distillery in 1833, produces a range of its own bottlings of different ages, as well as limited editions and specials for the travel market. It has a long, 110-hour fermentation process – the longest in Scotland, and it runs new make through the stills at a much slower rate than is usual. The distillery claims their craftsmanship is noticeable in its whisky.

Thanks to its proximity to Glasgow and Stirling, Glengoyne is a popular tourist attraction and its tours, of varying lengths, are always well subscribed.

**Address:** Dumgoyne by Killearn, G63 9LB
**Phone:** +44 1360 550254
**Web:** www.glengoyne.com

## Visitor Centre

The distillery is open to visitors from 10am to 5pm daily. A number of tours are offered, from one-hour tastings, to two-hour Malt Master tours, and even five-hour Masterclasses where you get to create your own Single Malt. There is also a shop to purchase Glengoyne products, and you can take a walk to the waterfall while visiting.

# Glenmorangie

Glenmorangie is perhaps one of Scotland's most loved distilleries and whiskies. What started out as a primitive farm distillery in 1843 slowly grew through the rest of the century, producing malts for blends. This continued into the 20th century under the ownership of Macdonald and Muir. They used it in Highland Queen and James Martin blends, although the distillery was mothballed during US prohibition and World War II.

Expansion came in the 1970s, with more stills added, and the introduction of a 10-year-old single malt. By 1983 this was the best selling single malt in Scotland, and thus began a love affair with this brand. It was therefore only a matter of time before big investment came, and in 2004 Moët Hennessy Louis Vuitton bought Glenmorangie for £300 million.

They set about giving it a more luxury appeal, tweaking everything from the branding to the names of its bottlings, to the shape of the bottles.

**Address:** A9, Tain, IV19 1PZ
**Phone:** +44 1862 892477
**Web:**
www.glenmorangie.com

## Visitor Centre

Full tours of the distillery, taking you through the different stages of whisky production, are offered at Glenmorangie. Open Monday to Friday (and weekends in summer), 10am to 5pm. There is a shop on site.

To distillery fans, Glenmorangie is notable due to it having the tallest stills in Scotland. They are 4.8m (over 16ft) in height, and mean the stillhouse is very tall (known as the Highland Cathedral). This has happened because the distillery started out producing gin, which uses tall stills. As they were gradually replaced, like-for-like models were brought in. This as a result creates a pure and light spirit. Combined with the wood finish of its barrels – another thing Glenmorangie is noteworthy for – their whisky is known to be high quality, and there are a number of experimental expressions tried out regularly.

Glenmorangie is also one of the growing number of distilleries turning to sustainable methods of production. Its wastewater is purified, and the waste draff and lees are converted into biogas for fuelling its energy needs.

# Glen Ord

If you know your whiskies, you may not have heard of Glen Ord. Founded in 1838 in the Black Isle peninsula, 15 miles west of Inverness, its main output is known as The Singleton. In fact, this whisky is produced almost entirely for the growing Asian market and thus is rarely spoken of in its home region. Its owners Diageo consider this an important distillery for its global reach, and as such its visitor centre is popular with tourists from the Far East.

Many of the original buildings from the 1800s survive, but the site has been added to with huge warehouses for its maltings and storage. Glen Ord distillery produces a huge 11 million litres per year using 14 stills. Aside from The Singleton, Glen Ord produces malt for Johnnie Walker blends.

**Address:** Glen Ord Distillery, Muir of Ord, Ross-shire, IV6 7UJ
**Phone:** +44 1463 872004
**Web:** www.malts.com/en-row/distilleries/the-singleton-of-glen-ord

## Visitor Centre

Guided tours of the distillery are offered, with tastings. Or you can try a tutored tasting experience in the dramming room. Open daily. Book through the website.

# The Glenturret

Could this be Scotland's oldest active distillery? The Glenturret would certainly make that claim, having been founded in 1775 and still going strong today. This whole area, hidden away in a valley near Crieff, was a source of illicit distilling, and this was one of the first in the area to go legal, paying the taxes due and avoiding the constant threat of the exciseman stopping the operation.

Today most whisky fans will know of The Glenturret's own single malts, which are highly regarded and well crafted. But this distillery has been one of the main suppliers of the malt which goes to create The Famous Grouse blend – one of Scotland's most famous whiskies. For years visitors came here to visit The Famous Grouse Experience visitor centre. But this closed in 2018 when the owners sold the distillery. Since then a new visitor centre aimed purely at The Glenturret and its own produce, as well as its history, has been opened and is well worth the visit.

The Glenturret sources its water from nearby Loch Turret, from where it gets its name. This water source is fed by Ben Chonzie, a mountain in the Grampians. Also notable is the fact this distillery still has a hand-operated mash – the only one still in use in Scotland.

There are a range of tours available to the visitor, plus a recently refurbished café and restaurant on site.

**Address:** The Hosh, Crieff PH7 4HA
**Phone:** +44 1764 656565
**Web:** www.theglenturret.com

## Visitor Centre

Take an immersive tour of Scotland's oldest working distillery. A range of tours, ranging from one hour to an entire day. The shorter tours run hourly from 10.30am and should be booked in advance where possible. Longer tours see you helping hand rouse the barley and even blend your own whiskey. Open Monday to Friday.

# Highland Park

Highland Park has the distinction of being Scotland's most northerly distillery. It should be noted that this is also one of the oldest in the country, having been granted a licence in 1798 when much of the country's whisky production was still illicit and behind closed (barn) doors.

The location of Highland Park on Orkney, near Kirkwall, has meant it always found difficulty in exporting its goods to mass market – particularly when it was prized by blenders in its earlier days. This in turn led to it being somewhat unknown until a serious effort began to market it to a wider audience in the late 1970s.

Today its single malt range, which extends up to 50-year-old bottlings, is highly regarded and was even prized by Winston Churchill.

The distillery still produces much of its own malt,

**Address:** Holm Road, Kirkwall, Orkney KW15 1SU
**Phone:** +44 1856 885604
**Web:** www.highlandparkwhisky.com

## Visitor Centre

Highland Park's visitor centre is a major attraction, with information about the distillery, its history and products. Four different tours are available, each looking around the distillery and enjoying a tasting. Some offer tastings of exclusive and heritage bottlings and gifts to take home. Booking is essential. There is a gift shop in the centre of Kirkwall. Open daily April to October, and Wednesday to Sunday, 10am to 5pm.

and farms peat from a bog nearby. Its stone buildings are traditional, with pagodas on top. Inside there are four stills, original maltings, and it has a capacity for 2.5 million litres per year. Its whisky is aged in both bourbon and sherry casks, giving a sweet and slightly smoky aroma and taste.

Thanks to increasing numbers of visitors to Orkney – particularly by cruise ship – Highland Park is now a major tourist attraction.

# Invergordon

A grain distillery in the Whyte & Mackay stable which opened in 1959. Invergordon is located on the Moray Firth and produces grain whisky for various blends. A single grain bottling was available until the 1990s.

**Visitor Centre**

No

**Address:** Golfview Ter, Invergordon IV18 0HP
**Phone:** +44 1349 852451
**Web:** www.whyteandmackayltd.com/our-locations/invergordon/

# Kingsbarns

Leading the way in the revival of the Lowlands whisky region, which at one point had dropped to just one distillery, is Kingsbarn.

Opened in 2015, it has created a purpose-built site and is taking its process seriously. Water is sourced from an aquifer underneath the distillery, and its barley is all grown in Fife. Maturation is done in carefully-selected casks from around the world. Two stills and four washbacks are used. The result is a complex and typically Lowland spirit which will soon be establishing itself in more aged bottlings.

In the meantime Kingsbarns offers a visitor experience and Founders' Club to keep informed with progress.

**Visitor Centre**

A purpose-built visitor centre invites you to learn more about Kingsbarns and its vision. You can visit the café and shop, and take a tour. These range from the introductory Kingsbarns Tour and 19th Hole Tour, to the more leisurely and informative Dream to Dram Tour. Booking is essential.

**Address:** East Newhall Farm, Kingsbarns, Fife KY16 8QE
**Phone:** +44 1333 451300
**Web:** www.kingsbarnsdistillery.com

# Jura

Jura is the island between Islay and the mainland, and the distillery here has existed since at least the 1830s. To many, its proximity to Islay should mean it is classified within that whisky region. However, Jura is considered a Highland distillery and its single malts are considered softer and sweeter than the heavy peated variants produced on its island neighbour.

Jura's distillery actually lay in ruin for over 50 years following a legal dispute between its owners and landlord. It was only in the 1950s that a new consortium purchased it, rebuilt the distillery and set about producing whisky on the island again in this new, non-peaty style (peaty limited edition bottlings have since been offered).

Today owned by the Emperador Distillers group and operated by Whyte & Mackay, Jura has grown to become some of the best-loved Scottish single malts.

**Address:** Craighouse, Isle of Jura PA60 7XT
**Phone:** +44 1496 820385
**Web:** www.jurawhisky.com

## Visitor Centre

Jura is a remote and sparsely populated place, but the Jura distillery is a beautiful place to visit. It offers tours of the distillery and a gift shop. Booking is recommended, particularly in the summer. Open Monday to Friday (plus Saturday in summer).

# Loch Lomond

Situated on the boundary between the Lowland and Highland whisky regions, Loch Lomond Distillery (situated near the southern shore of the loch itself) was opened in 1965, but distilling here goes back to 1772 when the Littlemill Distillery was founded. After many changes in ownership, today it is in private hands, producing both grain and malt whiskies.

While it produces its own extensive range of

**Address:** Lomond Estate, Bowie Road, Alexandria, Dunbartonshire G83 0TL
**Phone:** +44 1389 752781
**Web:** www.lochlomondwhiskies.com

## Visitor Centre

No

Loch Lomond single malt whiskies of various ages and styles, this distillery is also responsible for many smaller private label whisky brands, both single malts and blends. They include Clansman, Craiglodge, Croftengea, Dumbuck, Dunglass, Glen Catrine, Glen Douglas, Glen Scotia, Glengarry, High Commissioner, Inchfad, Inchmoan, Inchmurrin, Littlemill, Old Court, Old Original, Old Rhosdhu, Scotia Royale and Scots Earl. As you would expect, there is a large and extensive range of equipment, including 11 stills and a 30 million litre per annum capacity from this site. The uniqueness of the pot malt stills rests in the cylindrical necks of the spirit stills. Traditionally the necks of malt stills are open, whereas these include special distillation trays in the necks, allowing for greater contact with the cooling alcohol vapour. It makes the process more efficient. Loch Lomond also includes a large cooperage to ensure the quality of its casks – one of only four Scottish distilleries to include one.

# MacDuff

Founded in 1960, MacDuff is a Highland whisky distillery located at Banff, north of Aberdeen. Owned by Dewar's, it has grown to five stills, and released single malts under the Glen Deveron brand, as well as occasional MacDuff bottlings. Most of its produce is used in the William Lawson blend. No visitor tours offered.

**Visitor Centre**

No

**Address:** Banff, Aberdeenshire AB45 3JT
**Phone:** +44 1261 812612
**Web:** www.scotchwhisky.com/
whiskypedia/1880/macduff/

# Nc'nean

One of a new breed of whisky distilleries to have emerged in Scotland in recent years. Set up by Annabel Thomas, its aim is "to change the way the world thinks about whisky from Scotland. Her mission was to create a whisky which could exist in harmony with this planet we call home." Distilling of its single malt began in 2017 and it is available to buy now. It is produced from Scottish barley, and the distillery is powered by renewable energy, with 99.97% of waste being recycled.

Fermentation here takes 114 hours, and extra time is spent letting the barley take on its flavour. The whisky itself is matured in red wine and American oak barrels, giving it a sweetness. We suspect this is one to watch for the future.

**Visitor Centre**

Tours of Nc'nean are available for small parties and must be booked in advance. Come along and see how this innovative and new distillery approaches its work and operates in a sustainable way.

**Address:** Drimnin, By Lochaline, Morvern PA80 5XZ
**Phone:** +44 7593 581584
**Web:** www.ncnean.com

# Oban

Two businessmen founded a brewery in the small fishing port of Oban in 1793 and the next year turned their attention to distilling whisky. From that moment on, this site has continued producing whisky almost continuously to this day.

Oban town is now much bigger and built all around the distillery, meaning it remains small and only producing up to 700,000 litres per year. It is, nevertheless, well thought of and an important part of Diageo's stable.

Single malts have been produced here since the late 1970s, before it was as popular as it is today. Oban's various releases are popular and their 14-year-old joined the Classic Malts Selection in 1989. Today it also produces a range of special editions, including a recent *Game of Thrones* themed example.

Because of its small size, Oban has just two stills and rests them between runs to protect the purity and taste of their product. Their barley is fermented for five days for a richer flavour.

**Address:** Stafford Street, Oban, Argyll PA34 5NH
**Phone:** +44 1631 572004
**Web:** www.obanwhisky.com

## Visitor Centre

Tours of Oban's distillery are very popular. Knowledgeable guides uncover the ancient art of distilling, the history of the site, a look at the production, and end with a dram of the famous 14-year-old. Other, more exclusive tours are also available. Book through the website.

# Pulteney

Known universally as Old Pulteney, this small distillery in Wick was named in honour of Sir William Johnstone Pulteney who turned this sleepy little village into a major port in the herring industry.

For many years this was Scotland's most northerly mainland distillery and it used the growing port to import barley and export its whisky. Water is taken from Loch Hempriggs a couple of miles away, via a mill race.

For over 20 years Pulteney closed down when a local prohibition law was introduced. By the time it reopened the herring industry had all but gone, but still this brand of whisky went on to become award-winning many times over.

**Address:** Huddart St, Pulteney Distillery, Wick KW1 5BA
**Phone:** +44 1955 602371
**Web:** www.oldpulteney.com

## Visitor Centre

You can visit the shop and see some displays of the Pulteney distillery, or book on a tour which takes you around the compact rooms and offers tastings. Open Monday to Friday, and Saturdays in the Summer months.

# Royal Brackla

In order to sell more whisky and gain better recognition, Brackla's founder Captain William Fraser applied for a royal warrant. It was granted – the first distillery to get one – and thus it became Royal Brackla in 1833. Now owned by Bacardi with a huge output and modern buildings, it is not quite the same place, and part of the process is carried out elsewhere. But nevertheless, its own single malt range, dubbed 'The King's Own Whisky', is popular.

**Visitor Centre**
No

**Phone:** +44 1667 402002
**Web:** www.royalbrackla.com

# Royal Lochnagar

Royal Lochnagar in the Cairngorms was opened at New Lochnagar in 1845, named after the nearby mountain, and after the original Lochnagar distillery burned down. It gained its regal title in 1848 following a visit by Queen Victoria, who granted a Royal Warrant. Its proximity to her beloved Balmoral home was no doubt a useful tactic. It sources pure waters from the Scarnock springs.

The distillery produces malts for blends like Johnnie Walker. In the past it was a constituent of VAT 69. Today it remains a small distillery in fact, the smallest in the Diageo stable, with just one wash and one spirit still. It is, however, well thought of and continues to produce special edition single malts like its Distillers Edition, as well as its 12-year-old core bottling.

**Visitor Centre**
Tours of the distillery and an introduction to whisky making, followed by take-home samples of their 12-year-old, Distillery Edition and Selected Reserve bottlings, are available daily. Book ahead.

**Address:** Royal Lochnagar Distillery Balmoral, Crathie, Ballater, Aberdeenshire AB35 5TB
**Phone:** +44 1339 742700
**Web:** www.malts.com/en-row/distilleries/royal-lochnagar

# Scapa

Revived in 2004, Scapa dates back originally to 1885. It is one of two main distilleries in Orkney (Highland Park being the other) and uses a Lomond still for producing its whiskies. It had operated almost continuously until 1994 before being mothballed. Today five dedicated individuals maintain the distilling process.

You may be forgiven for thinking the Scapa distillery is a bit industrial and not totally befitting the wild landscape, but what it lacks in aesthetics it makes up for in its produce. The surroundings include the infamous Scapa Flow – a natural harbour used to shelter vessels from Viking times right up to the present day, and the site of the scuttling of the German Navy fleet following World War I.

A visit to this distillery involves a walk along the nearby seafront and the rugged coastline which is so spectacular. It also, naturally, involves tastings and a tour of the facility.

## Visitor Centre

Three different length tours take in the distillery and surroundings. Must be booked in advance.

**Address:** St Ola, Kirkwall, Orkney, KW15 1SE
**Phone:** +44 1856 876585
**Web:** scapawhisky.com

# Strathearn

Opened in 2013, Strathearn is part of a new wave of distilleries opening up in Scotland (and further afield) taking advantage of the craft movement in creating spirits. It is located on a converted farm in a beautiful location at Bachilton near Perth. Each year it releases a limited number of single casks filled with their spirit, but owing to its young age its main single malt product only dates from 2013 and 2014.

## Visitor Centre

No

**Address:** Bachilton Farm Steading, Methven PH1 3QX
**Phone:** +44 1738 840100
**Web:** www.strathearndistillery.com

# Talisker

Considering the size of Skye, it seemed unusual that so few distilleries survived there. In fact, only Talisker did until Torabhaig came along in 2017.

Talisker itself has existed since 1830. It struggled through much of its early existence, with poor sales, bankruptcy and poor infrastructure. Despite its waterside location, a pier was only constructed in 1900 to allow steamers to dock and deliver barley and take away barrels; prior to that they had to be floated out to the ship!

John Walker & Sons and John Dewar & Sons formed a consortium which purchased Talisker in 1916 and set about transforming it. It started providing whisky for Johnnie Walker Black Label, and the process of triple distilling was halted.

Today this rather utilitarian distillery, set in a wonderful backdrop, produces some of Scotland's finest whiskies. Its well-known peaty, smoky and peppery flavour is a result of the shape of its stills – some of which were reconstructed down to individual dents in the lyne arms following an explosion in 1960.

It is now owned by Diageo and produces many different age bottlings and limited edition expressions which all seem to hit the mark, win awards, and sell very well. The distillery is a popular tourist attraction on Skye.

**Address:** Carbost, Isle of Skye IV47 8SR
**Phone:** +1478 614308
**Web:** www.malts.com/en-row/distilleries/talisker

## Visitor Centre

Both introductory and more in-depth tours are offered at Talisker. These should be booked in advance to avoid disappointment. There's also a visitor centre, shop and bar on site.

# Teaninich

Mainly producing malts for blending, such as those used in Johnnie Walker Red Label, Teaninich also produces a couple of its own bottlings.

The distillery was built in the grounds of Teaninich Castle in 1817 and quickly grew its production. It changed hands numerous times, until expanded greatly in 1970, before closing in the early 1980s. Production resumed in 1991, with a mash filter installed in 2000 unlike other distilleries which use mash tuns.

**Address:** Riverside Drive, Alness IV17 0XB
**Phone:** +44 1349 885001
**Web:** www.malts.com/en-row/brands/teaninich

## Visitor Centre

No

# Tobermory

Tobermory's whisky bottles are usually branded with the date 1798, for this is when the site was first founded as the Ledaig Distillery by a local kelp dealer. However, between his death in 1837 and 1972, the distillery spent much of the time derelict or dormant, with only a brief period between 1916 and 1930 when the Distillers Company reinstated production.

Domecq resurrected Ledaig in the 1970s, bringing it up to modern standards with new equipment, but it was soon out of business and sold on again

**Address:** Tobermory, Isle of Mull, Argyll PA75 6NR
**Phone:** +44 1688 302647
**Web:** www.tobermorydistillery.com

## Visitor Centre

A shop and tasting experiences are available at the distillery, as well as online. Tours last 45 minutes, but there are different optional extras, such as tastings. Open daily. Bookings should be made in advance to avoid disappointment.

in the 1980s. Then Burn Stewart bought the site in 1991 and changed its name to that of the colourful town it is situated in.

Now producing gin alongside its fruity malts, and its peaty whisky which retains the Ledaig name. It is in full swing again and a popular visitor attraction. It is the only distillery operating on the Isle of Mull.

# Tomatin

Back in the 1970s, anyone with an interest in Scottish whisky would have pointed to Tomatin as the powerhouse of the industry. Producing 12 million litres per year from an industrial-scale site, it was the darling of the blenders thanks to its quality and capacity. But by 1984 this distillery was bankrupt and closed down.

Visiting Tomatin today, you might think it a strange place to build a distillery. Located a few miles north of what is nor the Cairngorms National Park, it is high up and remote from anywhere. But back in

**Address:** Tomatin, Inverness-shire IV13 7YT
**Phone:** +44 1463 248144
**Web:** www.tomatin.com

## Visitor Centre

Thanks to the modern A9 road, it's easier to visit Tomatin today. Its visitor centre has a gift shop and there are various tours on offer. Watch a film about the history of the distillery, and even bottle your own cask strength exclusive. Book online.

1897 when it was founded, it was deemed better to be situated close to the best source materials and use rail transport to get the product to market.

Following its 1984 demise, Tomatin became the first Scottish whisky distillery to be bought by a Japanese owner. Takara Shuzo Corp were customers of the distillery, so it made sense for them to rescue it and resuscitate the supply. In the process they downsized from 23 stills to the 12 in use today, and created a range of single malts and high quality blends which gained a reputation internationally. They include Tomatin Legacy, and the Cù Bòcan peated malt.

Tomatin    69

# Torabhaig

Torabhaig finally put an end to Talisker's dominance on the Isle of Skye, becoming only its second distillery to operate (legally) since the 1800s. Opened in 2017, it was the result of a long-term project started by the previous owner of the site who died prematurely. Mossburn Distillers purchased the site and converted this old farm into a modern distillery, using its produce for its blends. It is attracting visitors despite not having any single malts yet. The plan is to initially release a 10-year-old peated single malt, but we'll have to wait till the late 2020s to try it.

**Visitor Centre**

A small visitor centre, cafe and shop are available, with tours on request.

**Address:** Teangue, Sleat IV44 8RE
**Phone:** +44 1471 833447
**Web:** www.torabhaig.com

# Tullibardine

A distillery founded by a Welshman in 1949 using a former brewery site which as a history dating back to 1488. Tullibardine was owned by Whyte & Mackay before being mothballed in 1993. It was then bought and reopened in 2003, and sold again in 2011 to Picard Vins & Spiritueux. The distillery uses four stills and has a capacity of up to 2.7 million litres per annum, producing single malts aged in various styles of casks. The water source is particularly pure, filtering down from Danny Burn and the Ochil Hills.

**Visitor Centre**

A modern visitor centre offers various tours of Tullibardine daily from 10am to 4pm. Booking online in advance is recommended.

**Address:** Stirling Street, Tullibardine Distillery, Blackford, Auchterarder PH4 1QG
**Phone:** +44 1764 661809
**Web:** www.tullibardine.com

# Wolfburn

The most northerly distillery on mainland Scotland. It was originally founded in 1821 by William Smith and is named after the Wolf Burn which it takes its water from. Described as being in ruins by 1877, Worlfburn was finally revived in 2012. It has some young, but highly regarded, whiskies. Around 70% of its produce is being left to mature for older bottlings. Its industrial estate location is perhaps not inspiring, but tourist demand and Wolfburn's future potential has led to daily tours being offered.

inner workings of the distillery and its people at work. It doesn't have a visitor centre, so this is as authentic as it gets. Tastings are offered at the end of the tour, as well as a visit to the shop.

**Address:** Henderson Park, Thurso, Caithness KW14 7XW
**Phone:** +44 1847 891 051
**Web:** www.wolfburn.com

## Visitor Centre
Daily tours are offered at 2pm where you'll see the

*Tullibardine*

WOLFBURN DISTILLERY
652
THURSO
2013
WOLFBURN DISTILLERY
653
THURSO
2013
WOLFBURN DISTILLERY
THURSO
2013
684
THURSO
2013
685
WOLFBURN DISTILLERY
THURSO
2013
619
Wolfburn

*Kilchoman*

# ISLAY
## Whisky Region

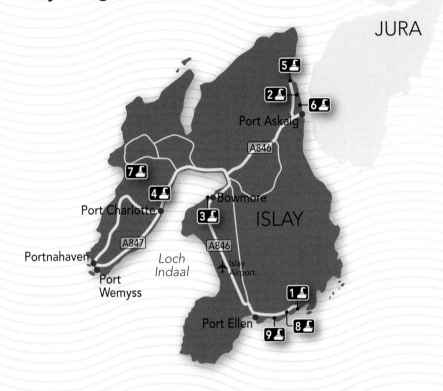

JURA

Port Askaig

A846

ISLAY

Bowmore

Port Charlotte

A847

Portnahaven

Port
Wemyss

Loch
Indaal

A846

Islay
Airport

Port Ellen

| 1. | ARDBEG | 4. | BRUICHLADDICH | 7. | KILCHOMAN |
|----|--------|----|----|----|----|
| 2. | ARDNAHOE | 5. | BUNNAHABHAIN | 8. | LAGAVULIN |
| 3. | BOWMORE | 6. | CAOL ILA | 9. | LAPHROAIG |

# Ardbeg

One of the three famous distilleries along Islay's southern shore, Ardbeg (alongside Lagavulin and Laphroaig) is known today for its distinctive peaty flavour, so common to this island.

Ardbeg is something of a survivor, or a late bloomer. It started life in 1815, but became a source of malt for blenders through much of its life. When supply started overstepping demand, its owners Allied Distilleries decided to mothball the site, leaving its buildings to fall into a very sorry state. But time wasn't up for this remote distillery, where the sea laps its warehouse at high tide. In 1997 it was brought back to life and upgraded by new owners Glenmorangie, who set about creating a range of single malt whiskies to showcase the popular Islay peat flavour.

With only two stills and a 1.25 million litre per annum output, Ardbeg is still a relatively small distillery. However, a number of its whiskies have gone on to win awards, and the brand has a loyal following. Visitors can enjoy the café, stay in the on-site holiday cottage, and

**Address:** Port Ellen, Islay PA42 7EA
**Phone:** +44 1496 302244
**Web:** www.ardbeg.com

## Visitor Centre

If you make it to this remote corner of Scotland, you'll be rewarded with incredible views, a wonderful café, and the chance to join a tour to discover how Ardbeg is made and sample a dram.

take tours of the distillery. Most importantly, you can join The Ardbeg Committee – a group of over 120,000 worldwide members who share one common purpose: "to celebrate the re-awakening of Ardbeg, spread the word and dispense drams to those deprived of knowledge of this untamed spirit."

# Ardnahoe

The newest of Islay's distilleries, opening in 2019. It is, as its website explains 'one Scottish family's dream unfolding as well as being the next chapter in the captivating story of the Whisky Isle of Islay.' Set up by Stuart Laing, a former employee of Bruichladdich, Ardnahoe is a family affair with his sons also taking up roles in the distillery. Its name means "Height of the Hollow", after the beautiful location in which its modern buildings are set. Loch Ardnahoe is the water source used in production, with two stills in a room with large, scenic vistas.

**Address:** Port Askaig, Isle of Islay PA46 7RU
**Phone:** +44 1496 840777
**Web:** www.ardnahoedistillery.com

## Visitor Centre

Open daily, with tours, a restaurant and fantastic views towards Jura. Take home a bottle of the spirit at the end of your tour. Best to book in advance.

Ardnahoe matures its spirit in both American oak bourbon and Jerez sherry barrels to give a full flavour. Its malt is, naturally, peaty and smoky as you would expect from Islay, but given the relative youth of Ardnahoe it is not ready yet!

A tour of the distillery is the best way to find out more about this new producer and their plans.

# Bowmore

Bowmore is the oldest distillery on Islay. It was founded by a local entrepreneur in 1779, and then rebuilt into its current form in 1840 after being sold to W & J Walker of Glasgow.

Today Bowmore is operated by Morrison Bowmore, which in turn is owned by Japanese giant Beam Suntory. It has a capacity of 2 million litres per year using four stills and six traditional wooden washbacks. It still uses a traditional malting floor and a peat-fired kiln, even though much of its barley is imported already malted. A former warehouse is now used as a public swimming pool, with water heated by waste heat from the distillery.

Bowmore's whisky is matured mostly in American oak casks, off site, with some finished in Sherry casks. Its single malts are typically peaty and smoky as you would expect from Islay, often with a salty and fruity taste. Its location is stunning and worth visiting. You can even stay in one of the holiday lets run by the distillery, situated in former worker cottages.

**Address:** School St, Bowmore, Isle of Islay PA43 7JS
**Phone:** +44 1496 810441
**Web:** www.bowmore.com

## Visitor Centre

There is a gift shop on site, and Bowmore offers a range of tours of the distillery, culminating in a dram in the Whisky Tasting Bar. Booking is essential. Open Tuesday to Saturday, 11am-4pm.

# Bruichladdich

Bruichladdich has one of Islay whisky's most interesting stories. Having been founded in 1881 the owners of the then-largest distillery in Scotland (Dundashill in Glasgow), they aimed to produce the popular, peaty Islay style whisky for use in blends. Its buildings and equipment were new and production began at a pace.

Then began a long rollercoaster ride for the distillery, seeing periods of closure, and many changes of ownership. In fact, when it closed in 1994 it looked like time had been called on Bruichladdich for good – until entrepreneurs stepped in to rescue it in 2000. The distillery was then given a new lease of life creating experimental bottlings, including Port Charlotte, which has become known as the peatiest whisky every produced. It also produces the smoky Octomore, named in honour of a lost Islay distillery.

Today Bruichladdich is owned by Remy Cointreau who have given it a boost and wider market, but also cut back on the experimental nature slightly. Nevertheless, this is a fascinating place which still uses the original Victorian buildings and equipment, which has all been lovingly restored. The distillery uses two wash and two spirit stills, with a single mashtun and six washbacks. Whisky is still produced and bottled by hand, with no automation involved.

**Address:** Bruichladdich Distillery, Isle of Islay, Argyll PA49 7UN
**Phone:** +44 1496 850190
**Web:** www.bruichladdich.com

## Visitor Centre

Take a tour of the distillery, learn about its history in the visitor centre, or enjoy refreshments and products in the gift shop. Open daily except Sunday.

# Caol Ila

With a shoreside location just outside Port Askaig, facing the island of Jura, Caol Ila's distillery is remarkably modern for its age. While it was founded in 1846, much of the site was demolished and rebuilt in the 1970s. Today it produces much of the blend that goes to make Johnnie Walker, but it is also gaining a reputation of its own thanks to the growing taste for Islay's whiskies.

Caol Ila's 12-year-old has won multiple awards, as do other expressions. All feature the typical Islay smokiness, but also offer sweetness and spices to balance it out.

There is a visitor experience at Caol Ila.

## Visitor Centre

Three different tours are offered, from a quick visit to the distillery and surroundings, to a luxury chocolate and whisky tasting, and a longer Cask Strength Experience where you can taste the rarer produce. The visitor experience is being improved in line with Caol Ila's growing prominence.

**Address:** Port Askaig, Isle of Islay PA46 7RL
**Phone** +44 1496 302769
**Web:** www.malts.com/en-row/distilleries/caol-ila

# Kilchoman

One of Islay's smaller distilleries, its only truly independent one, and the first to be built on Island in 124 years. Kilchoman is based on Rockside Farm and utilising barley grown on site, and water from a dam on the stream passing through the farm. It revives the idea of farm distilling, which was once the norm before commercialism took over the industry. It opened in 2005 and released its first 3-year-old single malt in 2009. A new visitor centre was opened in 2020. Further products were released at later dates as the spirit matured.

## Visitor Centre

Offers four different tours which should be booked in advance. Visit the distillery, learn about its history and vision, and sample its products.

Includes visitor centre, shop and café.

**Address:** Rockside Farm, Bruichladdich, Islay
**Phone:** +44 1496 850011
**Web:** kilchomandistillery.com

# Lagavulin

Now under the Diageo brand, Lagavulin is one of Islay's (and even Scotch whisky's) true survivors. Opened in the early 1800s, it initially supplied a shop in Glasgow owned by the distillery's owner. It went on to produce blends, like White Horse, and eventually producing its own single malts which quickly gained good reputation. In fact, so popular were the products that demand outstripped supply for a number of years.

The Lagavulin 16-year-old is probably the distillery's most popular among whisky fans, but there are younger bottlings to try (including a 9-year-old), and special releases like the Distillers Editions which add extra flavour. Like Laphroaig, Lagavulin is a peaty whisky as influenced by Islay itself. However, it is often easier to tackle than Laphroaig, with more sweetness and sherried flavour.

Situated between Ardbeg and Laphroaig on the south coast of Islay, it is an easy walk from Port Ellen, and you can take in the visitor centres of all three.

**Address:** Port Ellen, Islay PA42 7DZ
**Phone:** +44 1496 302749
**Web:** www.malts.com/en-row/distilleries/lagavulin

## Visitor Centre

Visitors can tour the distillery and watch Lagavulin being produced in the pear-shaped stills, and witness the slow maturation process. Three different length tours are available, and advance booking is required. Open daily, apart from Sundays in winter (and closed around Christmas and New Year).

# Laphroaig

One of the most distinctive and highly regarded Scottish whiskies, Laphroaig takes peat and smoke to new levels. Naturally these flavourings are expected given its Islay location, where peat bogs influence the taste of all the island's distilleries, but with Laphroaig there's a complex array of additional flavours, causing many to liken it to cough medicine, seaweed, soap and iodine. On paper it doesn't sound appealing, and many new to whisky find it hard to take to. But Laphroaig has many fans who consider it a true connoisseur's whisky. The distillery was founded in 1810, the same time as neighbouring Lagavulin, with the first bottles appearing in 1815. It has retained its floor maltings and manages a specialised process involving hand-cutting peat, cold-smoking kilns and varying the proportions of wood and carefully ageing the oak to produce its range of whiskies. These vary from the entry-level 10-year-old and Select to its older bottlings and special editions.

Laphroaig distillery is on the south side of Islay overlooking its own scenic little bay. The Kilbride Stream – a source of water and cooling for the distillery, flows down behind.

Taking advantage of its popularity and cult status, Laphroaig offers one of the best visitor experiences, taking guests through their process, history and large shop.

**Address:** Port Ellen, Islay PA42 7DU
**Phone:** +44 1496 302418
**Web:** www.laphroaig.com

## Visitor Centre

Open year round (usually closed Tuesday and Wednesday in the winter months), visitors can take a tour of the distillery, learn about the process and the history of Laphroaig, and indulge in their large shop selling all kinds of gifts. Of course, you can buy a bottle here, too, and knowledgeable staff will help you decide the best one to go for.

*The Clydeside Distillery*

# LOWLAND
## Whisky Region

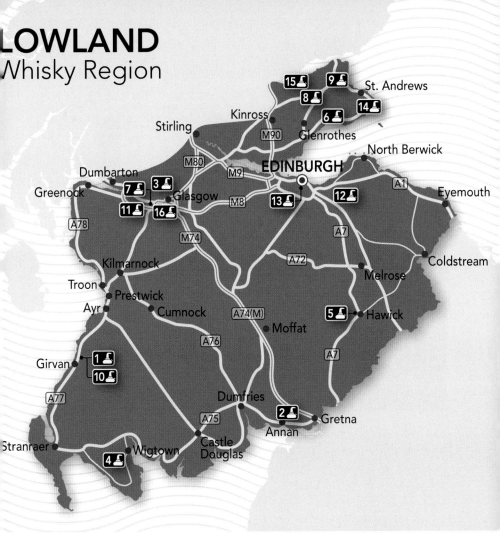

1. AILSA BAY
2. ANNANDALE
3. AUCHENTOSHAN
4. BLADNOCH
5. BORDERS DISTILLERY
6. CAMERONBRIDGE
7. THE CLYDESIDE DISTILLERY
8. DAFTMILL
9. EDEN MILL
10. GIRVAN
11. GLASGOW DISTILLERY
12. GLENKINCHIE
13. HOLYROOD
14. KINGSBARNS
15. LINDORES ABBEY
16. STRATHCLYDE

# Annandale

After a break of 96 years, whisky production returned to Annandale in Dumfries-shire when Professor David Thomson and Teresa Church opened their new distillery in 2014.

This is the closest Scottish whisky distillery to the English border and has already bottled its first 3-year-old single malts – both peated and unpeated - to rave reviews.

Annandale uses the original buildings from the first distillery here, which operated between 1830 and 1918, producing malt for Johnnie Walker. Prior to reopening it underwent a £10 million restoration and now includes a café and tours.

Annandale was one of the first distilleries in Scotland to pair-up one large wash still with two small spirit stills running in parallel. This greatly increases the ratio of surface area of copper to volume of liquid within the spirit stills, thereby encouraging copper complexing and the consequent precipitation of impurities. The resulting spirit is wonderfully smooth, even at cask filling strength.

As an independent distillery, Annandale is one to watch for the future.

**Address:** Northfield, Annan DG12 5LL
**Phone:** +44 1461 207817
**Web:** www. annandaledistillery.com

## Visitor Centre

Various tours are on offer, covering the history of the site and its rebirth, a discovery tour of the distilling process, and even personal tours by David Thomson himself. Open daily. Book on the Annandale website.

# Auchentoshan

One of the oldest distilleries in the area and, Auchentoshan was even for a while the sole surviving Lowland distillery until the recent revival. It dates from 1823, but there was an older distillery on the site and an even older brewery dating to the 1560s.

Situated in the ever expanding Clydebank to the west of Glasgow, Auchentoshan today is owne by Morrison Bowmore Distillers. It has three stills and draws water from Loch Katrine, as well as Loch Cochno for cooling. It produces 1.8 million litres per annum.

Auchentoshan approaches whisky making a little differently to others in Scotland. All of its malt is triple distilled, making its produce closer to Irish or American whiskeys than traditional Scotch. It has made it popular among those communities. This has made it a popular visitor attraction since the mid-2000s, thanks also to its proximity to Glasgow.

**Address:** Auchentoshan Distillery, By Dalmuir, Clydebank G81 4SJ
**Phone:** +44 1389 878561
**Web:** www.auchentoshan.com

## Visitor Centre

A visitor centre opened in 2005 offering guided tours of Auchentoshan's distillery and rounding it off with a dram and a visit to the gift shop. Open daily 10am to 5pm.

# Ailsa Bay

Sharing a site with Girvan distillery (see separate entry), Ailsa Bay is an industrial site with no visitor centre or tours. Yet its location, on the Firth of Clyde and looking out to Arran and Ailsa Craig, is spectacular. The distillery produces five different styles of whisky, contributing to blends such as Grant's, using modern-yet-traditional facilities. Its own Ailsa Bay Single Malt whisky is also made here and finding its place in the market.

**Visitor Centre**

No

**Address:** Grangestone Industrial Estate, Girvan, Ayrshire KA26 9PT
**Phone:** +44 1465 713091
**Web:** www.ailsabay.com

# Bladnoch

Located on the banks of the River Bladnoch, this Lowland distillery is the most southerly in Scotland. It was founded in 1817 and is tiny in size, with four stills currently in use. It was purchased in 2015 by an Australian entrepreneur. However, for much of its life it was restricted in its production by various owners, and spent periods mothballed with an uncertain future.

Today its new owners are celebrating this great little distillery and have opened a visitor centre and café. It produces award-winning single malts, as well as the Pure Scot blended whisky and various limited editions. Its flavours are light and grassy, typical of the Lowland region.

**Visitor Centre**

Opened in 2019, the visitor centre tells the story of this 200+ year old distillery and offers various tours. Booking is recommended. There is a café showcasing local produce.

**Address:** Bladnoch, Newton Stewart DG8 9AB
**Phone:** +44 1988 402605
**Web:** www.bladnoch.com

# The Borders Distillery

The Borders Distillery opened in 2018 and seems to be ticking all the right boxes. Founded by experienced whisky people, it has chosen a location where it stands out from the crowd, literally on the border with England. It has refurbished a traditional factory building and is aiming to be as environmentally friendly as possible. Hawick itself is a traditional mill

town with a growing tourist trade, and this should serve the distillery well as it grows and (literally) matures.

To date it is producing gins, vodkas, and blended whisky, with single malts on the horizon. It has installed four stills for the latter, with aged American and sherry oak barrels sourced for ageing.

**Visitor Centre**

Visitors can come and explore the highly-rated visitor centre and learn how The Borders Distillery is producing whisky (and other drinks), take a tour and buy something in the gift shop. Tours must be booked in advance.

**Address:** Commercial Rd, Hawick TD9 7AQ
**Phone:** +44 1450 374330
**Web:** www.thebordersdistillery.com

# Cameronbridge

Cameronbridge was the first distillery to produce grain whisky using Robert Stein's Column method. It opened in 1824. Today it is owned by Diageo and is an important constituent for its blends. It has been much upgraded and expanded, and even produces Gordon's gin and Smirnoff vodka at the site. It's most notable contribution is to David Beckham's Haig Club whisky.

**Visitor Centre**

No

**Address:** Windygates, Leven, Fife KY8 5RL
**Phone:** +44 1333 354061

# The Clydeside Distillery

Following The Glasgow Distillery, The Clydeside Distillery opened in 2017 and is also bringing whisky production back to the heart of Glasgow after decades of absence. It is located in the old Pumphouse at the entrance to Queen's Dock and it is producing a new Clydeside Single Malt whisky, distilling by hand in this historic setting. It has 2 stills at present and sources water from Loch Katrine.

**Visitor Centre**

The Clydeside includes a café, shop and you can book onto a range of tours to discover the distillery and its working areas, as well as enjoying a tasting session.

**Address:** 100 Stobcross Road, Glasgow G3 8QQ
**Phone:** +44 141 212 1401
**Web:** www.theclydeside.com

# Daftmill

Daftmill is a low-volume, small distillery located in a converted barn near Cupar in the Lowland region. It was founded in 2005 and uses two stills, water from its own well, produces its own grain, and releases a very limited number of bottles per year. A 12-year-old was released in 2018, as well as limited edition bottlings, and more are on the way.

**Visitor Centre**
No

**Address:** Daftmill Farm, by Cupar, Fife KY15 5RF
**Phone:** +44 1337 830303
**Web:** www.daftmill.com

# Eden Mill

A short distance north of St Andrews is this relatively new distillery. Occupying the site of a historic Haig distillery, where the crystal clear waters of the Eden Estuary were perfect for production, today's business was started as a brewery (beer was also traditionally brewed on this site by Seggie Brewery). Then the owners went into gin and whisky production, enamoured by the history of the place. Various early bottlings have been released while their single malts mature.

**Visitor Centre**
The Gatehouse in Guardbridge are where tastings and the visitor centre are located for the time being. This covers the beer, gin and whisky sides of the business.

**Address:** Main Street, Guardbridge, St Andrews, Fife KY16 0UU
**Phone:** +44 1334 834038
**Web:** www.edenmill.com

# Girvan

Girvan is one of Scotland's grain whisky distilleries and, sadly, its own bottlings are not very common. In fact, the distillery spends more time producing Hendrick's Gin, and it also shares its site with Ailsa Bay (see separate entry) and contributes to blends made at other distilleries. As such there are no visitor facilities and the site is quite industrial.

**Visitor Centre**

No

**Address:** Grangestone Industrial Estate, Girvan KA26 9PT
**Phone:** +44 1465 713091
**Web:** www.thegirvanpatentstill.com

# The Glasgow Distillery

Amazingly there had not been a whisky distillery in Glasgow for over a century when three businessmen set up The Glasgow Distillery in 2012. In fact, this is the latest incarnation of the name, with a previous Glasgow Distillery operating between 1770 and the early 1900s.
The distillery has invested in the best equipment, casks and ingredients to begin producing single malt whisky, using three stills (named after family members of the founders). While it waits for its whisky to mature, it has also produced a gin.

**Visitor Centre**

Tours of the distillery and available and can be booked online.

**Address:** 234 West George Street, Glasgow G2 4QY
**Phone:** +44 141 404 7191
**Web:** www.glasgowdistillery.com

# Holyrood

The first distillery to open in central Edinburgh for nearly a century, Holyrood is an interesting and exciting addition to the Scottish whisky-making scene. It emerged in 2019 and plans to create new whiskies with flavour and distinction, having enjoyed the chance to create their distillery in a brand new way.
To date only the whisky spirit is available to taste, but from the outset Holyrood has become a visitor experience to explore a working distillery and learn its methods. It is set in a Victorian railway building. It is also producing gin.

**Visitor Centre**

A tasting bar, gift shop and visitor tours are available. No need to book, but always advisable to check ahead.

**Address:** 19 St Leonard's Ln, Edinburgh EH8 9SH
**Phone:** +44 131 285 8977
**Web:** www.holyrooddistillery.co.uk

# Glenkinchie

Glenkinchie is close to Edinburgh, near the village of Pencaitland. It was founded in 1825 by two local farmers who tried to make a go of larger scale production from what they had (probably) been doing illegally on the side for years. It didn't always work, and the distillery spent time being used as a sawmill.

Revived in the late 1800s, its production methods were improved by new owners. Today it is owned by Diageo and produces whisky for Johnnie Walker blends. It also produces single malts, regularly regarded as among the best Lowland varieties.

**Address:** Pencaitland, Tranent, East Lothian EH34 5ET
**Phone:** +44 1875 342012
**Web:** www.malts.com/en-row/distilleries/glenkinchie

## Visitor Centre

As a fine example of a Victorian distillery, Glenkinchie is open to the public with a visitor centre in the old maltings. It acts as a museum to whisky distilling, and also has a fine restaurant and gift shop on site. Open daily, with direct buses from Edinburgh.

# Lagg

Arran's newest whisky distillery, producing its first spirit in 2019. For years illicit 'Arran Waters' were illegally smuggled from Lagg. Now this new distillery – which is fully legal, it might be added – is building on that heritage. It is producing peaty Arran whiskies using traditional methods, yet with modern standards, custom copper pot stills and four traditional washbacks.

Lagg's building offers something modern and different from the traditional construction seen at older distilleries, and incorporates a visitor centre and tour. The buildings have been designed to be sustainable and environmentally friendly, with a sedum blanket of plants across the roof which bloom with the seasons.

**Address:** Lagg Distillery, Kilmory, Isle of Arran KA27 8PG
**Phone:** +44 1770 870565
**Web:** www.laggwhisky.com

## Visitor Centre

You can join a tour of Lagg Distillery, learning about the history of illicit whisky production on Arran, and how they're building on that. Watch the production process, enjoy food in the cafe and visit the shop, which are open daily. Tours are daily, except Sunday and Monday in the winter. You can drop in for a shorter tour, or book in advance for the more detailed offering.

# Lindores Abbey

The ruined Lindores Abbey sits on the banks of the River Tay to the east of the small town of Newburgh. It is said that the first ever recorded whisky was distilled by one of the abbey's brothers in 1494, known as the water of life for its medicinal properties. Many a whisky afficionado might agree this is still true of the spirit today!

**Address:** Abbey Road, Newburgh, Fife KY14 6HH
**Phone:** +44 1337 842547
**Web:** www.lindoresabbeydistillery.com

## Visitor Centre

Visit the distillery, enjoy a drink in the bar, and learn of the important history of this site to Scottish whisky. You can book a tour of the distillery on the website.

The site is a scheduled ancient monument today, but since 2017 a visitor centre and small distillery has existed. With three stills and the first produce maturing, a 3-year-old should be released in 2021 with further aged bottlings to follow.

# Strathclyde

Built in 1927, Strathclyde in Glasgow is one of Scotland's biggest distilleries, with capacity for 40 million litres per annum. Always built to produce for blends, Strathclyde also produce grain whisky using two stills, and the remaining five produce neutral spirit. Only rare single malt bottlings have ever been produced.

**Visitor Centre**
No

**Address:** 40 Moffat Street, Glasgow G5 0QB
**Phone:** +44 141 429 2024

# SPEYSIDE
## Whisky Region

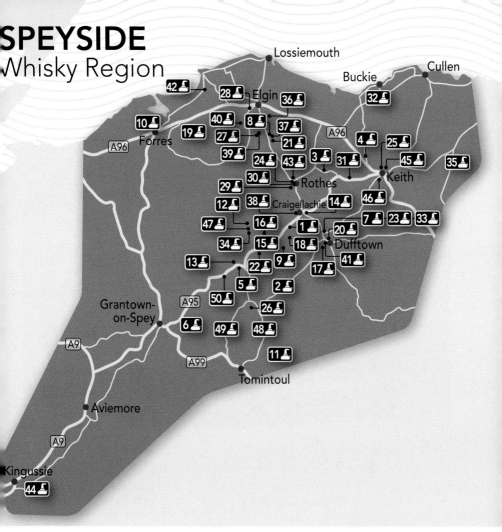

| | | |
|---|---|---|
| 1. | ABERLOUR | |
| 2. | ALLT A'BHAINNE | |
| 3. | AUCHROISK | |
| 4. | AULTMORE | |
| 5. | BALLINDALLOCH | |
| 6. | BALMENACH | |
| 7. | BALVENIE, THE | |
| 8. | BENRIACH | |
| 9. | BENRINNES | |
| 10. | BENROMACH | |
| 11. | BRAEVAL | |
| 12. | CARDHU | |
| 13. | CRAGGANMORE | |
| 14. | CRAIGELLACHIE | |
| 15. | DAILUAINE | |
| 16. | DALMUNACH | |
| 17. | DUFFTOWN | |
| 18. | GLENALLACHIE | |
| 19. | GLENBURGIE | |
| 20. | GLENDULLAN | |
| 21. | GLEN ELGIN | |
| 22. | GLENFARCLAS | |
| 23. | GLENFIDDICH | |
| 24. | GLEN GRANT | |
| 25. | GLEN KEITH | |
| 26. | GLENLIVET, THE | |
| 27. | GLENLOSSIE | |
| 28. | GLEN MORAY | |
| 29. | GLENROTHES | |
| 30. | GLEN SPEY | |
| 31. | GLENTAUCHERS Chivas Brothers Ltd | |
| 32. | INCHGOWER | |
| 33. | KININVIE | |
| 34. | KNOCKANDO | |
| 35. | KNOCKDHU | |
| 36. | LINKWOOD | |
| 37. | LONGMORN | |
| 38. | MACALLAN, THE | |
| 39. | MANNOCHMORE | |
| 40. | MILTONDUFF | |
| 41. | MORTLACH | |
| 42. | ROSEISLE | |
| 43. | SPEYBURN | |
| 44. | SPEYSIDE | |
| 45. | STRATHISLA | |
| 46. | STRATHMILL | |
| 47. | TAMDHU | |
| 48. | TAMNAVULIN-GLENLIVET | |
| 49. | TOMINTOUL | |
| 50. | TORMORE | |

# Aberlour

Another of Scotland's great whisky distillery visitor centres can be found at Aberlour. This time more for serious whisky fans, it makes an interesting diversion with decent length tours.

Aberlour was founded in the village of the same name in 1826, but moved to is current site a little outside in 1879. Its source is the pure rainwater from the Ben Rinnes mountain range which filters to local springs. The buildings are traditional Victorian in style and include four stills.

The distillery has always produced blends, but also saves around half of its production for its single malts which are popular particularly in Europe. The flavour from ageing in oak barrels is finished off by a period in sherry barrels, which makes Aberlour particularly appealing in France.

**Address:** Banffshire, A95, Aberlour AB38 9PJ
**Phone:** +44 1340 8811249
**Web:** www.aberlour.com

## Visitor Centre

The modern visitor centre opened in 2002 and is open Wednesday to Sunday from 10am-12pm and 2-4pm. Tours and tastings are offered, aimed more at connoisseurs and lasting up to two hours. Book through the Aberlour website.

# Allt-á-Bhainne

Allt-á-Bhainne owes its existence to Chivas Regal. The popular blend grew in popularity in the 1970s and this distillery in Moray was built entirely to produce the whisky needed in its creation. The name means 'milk burn', after its water source. It uses four stills and produces up to 4.2 million litres per annum, with occasional bottlings of its own single malts.

**Visitor Centre**

No

**Address:** Glenrinnes, Moray AB55 4DB
**Phone:** +44 1542 783200
**Web:** www.allt-a-bhainne.com

# Auchrosik

Auchroisk was founded in 1972 with a modern distillery and facilities, but using the ancient Dorie's Well as a source of water. Its main purpose is providing malt for the J&B blended whisky. However, it did produce its own single malt, named The Singleton (since no-one could pronounce Auchroisk), since abandoned. The distillery is not open to the public.

**Visitor Centre**

No

**Address:** Mulben, Moray AB55 6XS
**Phone:** +44 1542 860333
**Web:** www.malts.com/en-gb/brands/auchroisk

# Aultmore

Despite a heritage dating back to 1895, Aultmore distillery today is much more modern affair. Many of the distillery's buildings were upgraded or added in the 1970s, and this place is still busy with the serious business of producing whisky for blends. However, it has also been growing its single malt range under the ownership of Bacardi since 1998, with many fans.

**Visitor Centre**

No

**Address:** Aultmore, Moray AB55 6QY
**Phone:** +44 1542 881800
**Web:** www.aultmore.com

# Ballindalloch

Created inside derelict 19th century farm buildings on the Ballindalloch Castle estate in Speyside, this new distillery began producing in 2014 and is still going through maturation. This is a hands-on affair, with a 'single estate' nature, producing barley on site and taking water from nearby Garline Springs.

## Visitor Centre

Visitors who call ahead are welcome to come and see the distillery and learn about its creation and what is to come, subject to availability.

**Address:** Ballindalloch AB37 9AA
**Phone:** +44 1807 500331
**Web:** www.ballindallochdistillery.com

# Balmenach

Founded in 1824, Balmenach is one of Scotland's oldest legal distilliers. It was founded the year after licencing came into force, and stayed in the McGregor family for a hundred years. It is now owned by International Beveridge Holdings. With a source from the Cromdale Hills, the distillery has 6 stills and 2 million litres per annum output. Apart from a limited bottling, it only produces whisky for blends.

## Visitor Centre

No

**Address:** Balmenach Road, Cromdale, Moray PH26 3PF
**Phone:** +44 1479 872569

# The Balvenie

Dufftown has one of the highest concentrations of whisky distilleries in all of Scotland. This location at the heart of Scotland sees The Balvenue practically sharing the same spot as Glenfiddich, with many others close by.

Founded in 1886 in a ruined castle, with second-hand stills, Balvenie has grown into a major brand even with its more famous neighbour literally overshadowing.

The Balvenie is one of the only Distilleries in Scotland that grows its own barley, uses traditional floor maltings, employs coopers to tend to the casks and a coppersmith to maintain the stills on site. Plus, David C. Stewart MBE is the company's Malt Master, and considered one of the best in the business.

**Address:** Dufftown, Keith AB55 4BB
**Phone:** +44 1340 822 210
**Web:**
www.thebalvenie.com

## Visitor Centre

Nestled in the picturesque surroundings of Dufftown, Speyside, you will see the only traditional, working floor maltings in the Scottish Highlands; meet some of the expert craftsmen; and nose and taste some of their finest whisky. Tours of The Balvenie are limited to 8 persons, and must be booked in advance. They run three times per day, and cost £50. Bottling your own whisky has an additional cost.

His ground-breaking method of 'double casking' – a practice perfected at The Balvenie by taking whisky from traditional ex-bourbon American oak casks and then moving it to ex- Oloroso sherry Spanish oak casks to 'finish' the liquid, creating an unmistakable flavour. This is a method used by many other distilleries, but began here and is honoured in The Balvenie's Doublewood single malt. This is one of many whiskies in its core range, and these are supplemented by a range of limited editions, travel exclusives and rare bottlings.

The distillery left the grounds of the ruined Balvenie Castle in 1893 when an old mansion was converted. Since then the site has grown, but retained a lot of this history and character.

# BenRiach

BenRiach has one of the most interesting histories of all Speyside's many distilleries. Originally founded in 1897, it had already gone bankrupt by 1899 and closed down by 1903 after takeover by Longmorn.

Revived in 1965 to use its stills for producing peated whisky for Islay's Seagram distillery, until 2004 when new owners finally came on board to give BenRiach the recognition it deserves by producing their own bottlings using the stocks which remained from the years of fragmented production. Thanks to the peaty history, it has

**Address:** The Benriach Distillery, Elgin IV30 8SJ
**Phone:** +44 1343 862888
**Web:** www.benriachdistillery.com

## Visitor Centre

Tours and a shop offer a chance to sample BenRiach's products and learn about the process and history of this distillery. Book through their website.

meant BenRiach's whiskies are the only Speyside malts with such west coast flavours.

The distillery is built on the former Riach farm in a rich whisky producing area, close to Longmorn and south of Elgin.

BenRiach has one of the most interesting histories of all Speyside's many distilleries. Originally founded in 1897, it had already gone bankrupt by 1899 and closed down by 1903 after takeover by Longmorn.

Revived in 1965 to use its stills for producing peated whisky for Islay's Seagram distillery, until 2004 when new owners finally came on board to give BenRiach the recognition it deserves by producing their own bottlings using the stocks which remained from the years of fragmented production. Thanks to the peaty history, it has meant BenRiach's whiskies are the only Speyside malts with such west coast flavours.

The distillery is built on the former Riach farm in a rich whisky producing area, close to Longmorn and south of Elgin.

# Benrinnes

A 1950s-era distillery complex near Aberlour which operates six stills, producing whisky for blends. It actually has a heritage dating back to 1826 when founded on a different site which was later washed away, and an older building on the current site which burnt down in 1896. For a while Benrinnes used a partial triple distillation process before reverting to more traditional methods in 2007. Its own 15-year-old single malt is popular.

**Visitor Centre**
No

**Address:** Aberlour, Banffshire, AB38 9NN
**Phone:** +44 1340 871215
**Web:** www.malts.com/en-gb/brands/benrinnes

# Benromach

Benromach is one of Speyside's smaller distilleries and has fought hard to return to its current position following a turbulent early history. It was founded in 1898 and was sold to new owners a number of times until, in 1983, it was finally closed and had all equipment removed. It seemed like the end was nigh.

Yet in 1993, Gordon & MacPhail bought Benromach and set about reviving it. It's still small, but it has a loyal following, and an interesting visitor experience. And, of course, it has excellent single malts.

With the Romach Hills supplying the spring water, its two stills work hard to produce around 400,000 litres per annum. Most of its whiskies are peaty, and it even produces a Soil Association-certified Organic single malt.

**Visitor Centre**
Benromach Distillery has a Visitor Centre and gift shop. Tours of the distillery are available, as well as tastings, and in recent times 'virtual tours' have been on offer via the Benromach website.

**Address:** Invererne Rd, Forres IV36 3EB
**Phone:** +44 1309 675968
**Web:** www.benromach.com

# Braeval

Part of Chivas Brothers, Braeval is a private distillery in Banffshire which has five stills. It was opened in 1974, but mothballed from 2001-2008. Its own bottlings are rare and sought after.

Today Braeval is in the business of producing blending material for its owners. It is not open to the public.

**Visitor Centre**

No

**Address:** Braeval Distillery, Chapeltown, Moray AB37 9JS
**Phone:** +44 1542 783042

# Cardhu

Named after the farm on which John and Helen Cummings were illegally producing whisky in the 1811, Cardhu later gained a licence and was soon sold to Johnnie Walker who used its produce to create its various blends.

The Cummings family continued to run the distillery until the Second World War, having invested in a new site and new stills prior to the sale to Johnnie Walker. Cardhu uses a source of spring water which rises through peat to give it a unique flavour.

Cardhu's own single-malts have long been popular in Spain, and owing to supply issues a blend was created which was labelled 'Pure Malt' to avoid cheapening the product. This led to one of Scottish whiskey's biggest scandals, which was even debated in parliament before the product reverted to an actual single malt again.

While Johnnie Walker fans will continue to taste Cardhu in this drink, the distillery's own single malts are gaining a good reputation. Its 12-year-old is the main bottling.

**Address:** Knockando, Aberlour AB38 7RY
**Phone:** +44 1479 874635
**Web:** www.malts.com/en-row/distilleries/cardhu

## Visitor Centre

A visitor centre and gift shop is available at Cardhu. Learn the story of the distillery, its famous woman founded, and take a tour of the production areas to discover how it is made. Views of the surroundings from the distillery are lovely.

# Cragganmore

Cragganmore has a quiet reputation, but is well liked by connoisseurs and was even chosen by owner Diageo to be showcased in its Classic Malts range in 1998. For a Speyside distillery, its whisky is considered quite complex.

Founded in 1869 by experienced distiller John Smith, he had the foresight to build close to the Craggan burn (from where it takes its name) as a source of water and power, with good barley and peat for its flavouring nearby. It was also the first Scottish distillery to build a railway siding to allow its products to be distributed by rail. Still a small distillery today, with just two wash and two flat-topped spirit stills, and an output of around 1.5 million litres per annum, its core release is a 12-year-old single malt, with some special editions to note.

Tours are available of Cragganmore.

**Address:** Cragganmore Distillery Ballindalloch, Banffshire AB37 9AB
**Phone:** +44 1479 874715
**Web:** www.malts.com/en-row/distilleries/cragganmore

## Visitor Centre

Various tours of the distillery, with tasting, ranging from 45 to 90 minutes, are available Monday to Saturday, 10am to 5pm, between March and October. Booking is essential.

# Craigellachie

At the heart of Speyside in Aberlour. Craigellachi, opened in 1891, is operated by Dewar's on behalf of owner Bacardi. It primarily produces malt for Dewar's blends, but has also released some of its own single malts with odd ages, like its 13-, 17-, 19-, and 23-year-old limited bottlings. Its produce is renowned for its robust, pineapple tones. Not open to the public.

**Visitor Centre**

No

**Address:** Hill St, Craigellachie, Aberlour AB38 9ST
**Phone:** +44 1340 872971
**Web:** www.craigellachie.com

# Dailuaine

Opened in 1852 and rebuilt in 1889, Dailuaine produces malt for blends under ownership of Diageo. Its own single malt bottlings are very rare. Nevertheless, this distillery, which pioneered the pagoda style roof to draw smoke through the malt, produces over 3.3 million litres per annum.

**Visitor Centre**

No

**Address:** Carron, Aberlour, Moray AB38 7RE
**Phone** +44 1340 872500
**Web:** www.malts.com/en-gb/brands/dailuaine

# Dalmunach

Dalmunach is a modern distillery, opened in 2015 on the site of the demolished Imperial Distillery in Carron. It has embraced technology and is home to 16 shiny washbacks and giant mashtun made recently. There are, however, hints to the design of the lost Imperial in the buildings of Dalmunach. This state-of-the art distillery produces up to 10 million litres per annum, used in blends.

**Visitor Centre**

No

**Address:** Dalmunach Distillery, Carron, Moray AB38 7QP

# Dufftown

Dufftown as a place is known as the spiritual heart of Speyside whisky production. There are a number of distilleries here, but only one bears its name. Opened in 1895 as Dufftown-Glenlivet Distillery, it is a producer of malt for blends such as Bells – something it has done since the early 1900s when owned by Arthur Bell & Sons. Today Diageo owns Dufftown, operating six stills and 12 washbacks to keep production levels high.

**Visitor Centre**

No

**Address:** Dufftown, Moray AB55 4BR
**Phone:** +44 1340 822100

# GlenAllachie

Only established in 1967, The GlenAllachie was recently taken over by master distiller Billy Walker from previous owners Chivas Brothers, bucking the recent trend. It has a growing core range of whiskies along with limited edition and special bottlings.

It sits on the Beachschach Burn which provides water directly to the distillery and, with mighty Ben Rinnes standing tall behind, it really is a lovely setting.

In terms of its production, GlenAllachie recently increased its capacity to four million litres per year, but doesn't actually achieve this amount yet. The team instead focus on longer fermentation of 160 hours to help them 'discover the character and make of the new make spirit.'

It uses two separate spirit safes with a set of stills each, and was able to acquire a stock of aged 1970s barrels when it became independent. The distillery releases occasional limited bottlings, Wood Finishes, Single Casks on top of its core range.

GlenAllachie is building on its independent nature and was awarded Scottish Distillery of the Year in 2019 at the Scottish Whisky Awards. Its recently-opened visitor centre gives guests the chance to learn more about them and what they are building.

**Address:** Aberlour, Banffshire, AB38 9LR
**Phone:** +44 1340 872547
**Web:** www.theglenallachie.com

## Visitor Centre

The GlenAllachie visitor centre opened fairly recently and offers two experiences. Both give a tour of the distillery and a chance to speak to staff. The first runs 10am and 1pm Monday to Friday and lets you sample four whiskies. The second, running at 11.30am and 2.30pm Monday to Friday includes sampling an exclusive hand-fill not available elsewhere. You can book online.

# Glenburgie

Glenburgie has had an interesting history, changing name from Kilnflat in 1829, changing ownership various times, and even being completely rebuilt in 2004. It is now quite state-of-the-art, but retains the two original stills (with a third added, too). The distillery is not open to the public, and provides whisky for Ballantine's blend. Its own bottlings are rare, limited editions.

**Visitor Centre**

No

**Address:** Forres, Moray, IV36 2QY
**Phone:** +44 1343 554120

# Glendullan

Currently owned by Diageo, Glendullan opened in 1897 as the seventh (and last) in Dufftown. It produced whisky for blends, which it continues doing today, although Singleton of Glendullan single malt bottlings are available as exports. The current distillery superseded the original buildings in 1972. It has 6 stills and uses Conval Hill springs as a water source for its non-peaky whisky.

**Visitor Centre**

No

**Address:** Dufftown, Moray AB55 4DJ
**Phone:** +44 1340 822300

# Glen Elgin

Just 10 miles from the mouth of the River Lossie, Glen Elgin is a Speyside distillery not as widely known as some of its neighbours. Opened in 1898 to capitalise on the demand for blends, it has always had an up-and-down nature. It was sold in 1930 and is now owned by Diageo, using it to contribute to White Horse. It has been expanded to 6 stills, but still underwent mothballed periods in the 1990s. It now also produces single malts under its own name, and continues to hand-make its whisky without computerisation.

**Visitor Centre**

No

**Address:** Glen Elgin Road, Longmorn, Moray IV30 8SL
**Phone:** +44 1343 862100
**Web:** www.malts.com/en-gb/brands/glen-elgin

# Glenfarclas

Truly one of the big names in Scottish whisky, and a well-known family firm which produces one of the most enduring ranges of whiskies.

Set at the heart of Speyside in Ballindalloch, Glenfarclas has been in the Grant family since John bought it in 1865. Initially leased to John Smith of Cragganmore fame, John Grant later installed his son George as the distillery and the farm it was situated on. It carried on through the family, via George's widow, and then his children and later generations, growing to become what it is today. It is a rare example of a large distillery not owned by a multi-national firm.

Glenfarclas is fed from the heather and snow covered slopes of Ben Rinnes which rises behind the distillery. Its excellent taste is the result of

**Address:** Ballindalloch, Banffshire, AB37 9BD
**Phone:** +44 1807 500345
**Web:** www.glenfarclas.com

## Visitor Centre

Three different tours are on offer year-round at the visitor centre, with the Classic Tour offering an insight into the history of the distillery, its production process, a tasting in the Ship's Room (featuring panelling from the RMS Empress of Australia) and a visit to the shop. The more in depth Connoisseur's Tour and Five Decades Tour both take in more of the site, its warehouses, and samples of rarer whiskies from the range. Booking and times available on the website.

twice-distilling, and the use of sherry casks from Spain, rather than the more usual bourbon barrels. There are six stills (though not all are in constant use), and the distillery has a capacity of 3.5 million litres of spirit per year. Almost 70,000 casks are to be found maturing in the many warehouses on site. A visitor centre was opened in 1973, long before whisky tourism became big business. Tours offer visitors an insight into this family-run business and the whiskies it produces, from the standard range, to the famous Glenfarclas 105 Cask Strength, and the Family Casks range.

# Glenfiddich

The best known of all the whisky brands and distillers in Scotland, Glenfiddich is a tale of determination and self reliance which has resulted in it becoming one of the world's largest producers.

Glenfiddich was the best-selling single malt whisky for over 40 years until recently overtaken by The Glenlivet. Yet with such large numbers of sales still today, second place is nothing to be sniffed at. This distillery, in the Speyside whisky hotbed that is Dufftown, was also the first to open a visitor attraction in 1969 – something that wouldn't be possible without a wide following for its products.

Started in 1886 by William Grant, a former soldier and employee at Mortlach Distillery, Glenfiddich began life with old stills and buildings put up by hand. But it worked, by producing spirit that was sold to blenders and a developing a determination to make his business successful.

Glenfiddich began producing its single malts in the 1960s, which was a smart move as it began the public's love affair with the drink and helped it become the best-selling bottle. It was so popular that the distillery was expanded in 1974 to 31 stills. Today it has 32, and produces up to 14 million litres per annum.

**Address:** Dufftown, Keith AB55 4DH
**Phone:** +44 1340 820373
**Web:** www.glenfiddich.com

## Visitor Centre

Visitors to the distillery's revamped £2 million visitor centre will learn of its history, production methods, and products. Enjoy tutored tasting sessions, meals, afternoon teas, gifts and of course guided tours. It makes a great day out.

# Glen Grant

According to legend, grain merchant John Grant was a supplier to the illegal distilleries operating around Aberlour in the 1830s. Inspired by the opportunities, he leased the original Aberlour distillery with his brother, solicitor James Grant, and in 1840 set up their own distillery. It was supplied with water from Glen Grant burn, which also powered the machinery.

The local railway came steaming through in 1851, and a siding was built to serve Glen Grant. Then, in 1861, it became the first to use electric lighting in the Highlands. Under the ownership of James Grant's eccentric son "The Major", Glen Grant grew into the world's most famous whisky brand by the 1930s. He developed the Victorian Gardens behind the distillery.

The Grant family retained ownership until 1977 when it was sold to Seagrams. Later it was owned by Pernod Ricard, and today is part of Gruppo Campari, thanks in no small part to the popularity of its whisky in Italy. In fact, Glen Grant is one of the best-selling single malts in international markets.

Glen Grant's buildings are among the most elegant of Scotland's distilleries. They feature pepper pot turrets and sandstone walls. Inside, four stills produce almost 6 million litres per annum. Since 2008 a visitor centre has been open.

**Address:** Glen Grant Distillery Elgin, Rothes, Aberlour AB38 7BS
**Phone:** +44 1340 832118
**Web:** www.glengrant.com

## Visitor Centre

The Glen Grant Distillery and Victorian Gardens are open to visitors, with a shop and tours on offer. Open Monday to Saturday from 10am to 3pm.

# The Glenlivet

The Glenlivet is one of the big names in Scottish whisky. In fact, today this is the best-selling single malt brand, having overtaken Glenfiddich in 2014. Situated in the wild and remote Livet Valley, which is a part of Speyside where whisky making has a long history. When George Smith began distilling here, he was likely one of the more than 200 people doing it illegally. However, when he founded Glenlivet in 1824, he secured a licence and began producing legally – which did not make him popular among his local contemporaries.

Initially producing for blended malts keen for the 'Glenlivet style' it is today part of big name producers Pernod Ricard under their Chivas Brothers division and produces a range of many core single malt bottlings. Some of its produce does still go into Chivas Regal and Royal Salute blends

The Glenlivet's water source is Josie's Well and Blairfindy Well, and with 14 copper pot stills, it has a large capacity of 10.5 million litres per annum. The distillery was expanded and upgraded in 2010.

**Address:** Glenlivet, Ballindalloch AB37 9DB
**Phone:** +44 1340 821720
**Web:** www.theglenlivet.com

## Visitor Centre

Visit Glenlivet and enjoy a tour of the distillery, a dram in the library, or the chance to buy a special expression and other items from the gift shop. Signposted walks lead through the Livet Valley where you can discover the history of illicit distilling here. Pre-booking is essential for tasting tours. Distillery is open daily from March to November. Open Tuesday-Saturday December to February.

Glen Keith

# Glen Keith

A distillery opened in 1957 with the purpose of supplying malts for the blends of its owners, Seagram. It is today owned by Chivas Brothers. Glen Keith introduced computer technology long before other distilleries, and today produces up to 6 million litres per annum via 6 stills and 15 washbacks. It has used both triple and double distillation techniques.

Closed for a while in the early 2000s, it is now back in full swing. Sadly single malt bottlings are very rare.

**Address:** Station Road, Keith, Moray AB55 5BU
**Phone:** +44 1542 783044

**Visitor Centre**
No

# Glenlossie

Established in 1876, Glenlossie shares a site and employees with Mannochmore distillery (see separate entry) which was built later. It has no visitor facilities and mostly produces whisky for blends for its owners Diageo, with rare bottlings as a single malt. Uses six stills fitted with purifier pipes to carry heavier alcohols back for redistilling.

**Visitor Centre**
No

**Address:** Glenlossie Rd, Thomshill, Elgin IV30 8ST
**Phone:** +44 1343 862000

# Glen Moray

Glen Moray has been producing whisky since it was converted from a brewery in 1897, but spent much of its early life in the shadow of Glenmorangie and Ardbeg, the two better-known distilleries under the same ownership. It was always used to produce malt for blends, even when sold to La Martinique who use it today for their Label 5 whisky.

Nevertheless, Glen Moray, does produce its own single malts, both peated and classic light Speyside varieties. It takes its process seriously, creating whisky by hand. Being the only distillery in Elgin has led to the opening of a visitor centre.

**Address:** Bruceland Road, Elgin, Moray IV30 1YE
**Phone:** +44 1343 550900
**Web:** www.glenmoray.com

## Visitor Centre

The small visitor centre welcomes visitors to come and join a tour of the distillery or a tasting. Four tours are offered each day, with separate whisky tastings offered. Open Monday to Friday (and Saturday in the summer). Must be booked in advance.

# The Glenrothes

Like many of the distilleries in this part of Speyside, they are hidden away out of sight so you can easily pass by without noticing them. The Glenrothes was founded on the wave of new distilleries popping up across the region, with two businessmen taking a chance on this one which was constructed in 1878.

Its malt is primarily used in the Cutty Sark blend among others. But the quality of its produce has also led to a number of single malt bottlings between the 1970s and 1990s, all of which sold out quickly. A number of new single malts of different ages are available today.

**Visitor Centre**

No

**Address:** Glenrothes Distillery, Rothes, Morayshire, AB38 7AA
**Phone:** +44 1340 872300
**Web:** www.theglenrothes.com

# Glen Spey

Glen Spey, in Morayshire at the heart of the Speyside region, was founded in 1878. Today it is owned by Diageo and primarily produces product for J&B blended whisky, with a 1.4 million litre capacity per year. It was expanded in the 1970s. Its own main product is Flora & Fauna, but it has also produced a number of special and limited editions over the years.

**Visitor Centre**

No

**Address:** Glen Spey Distillery, Rothes, AB38 7AT
**Phone:** +44 1340 831215

# Glentauchers

Dating from 1897, Glentauchers always had the remit to provide malts for blends. Its founder owner James Buchanan used it to supply the Black & White whisky, and given the distillery's site next to the main railway line, was able to transport produce easily in the early days of the railways. Not open to the public, you might find a rare Glentauchers single malt bottling from the 1990s if you look hard enough.

**Visitor Centre**

No

**Address:** Mulben, Moray AB55 6YL
**Phone:** +44 1542 860272

# Inchgower

A Speyside distillery at Buckie, near where the Spey meets the sea. Founded in 1871 with second-hand equipment from the closed-down Tochineal Distillery. It was owned by Arthur Bell & Sons for many years, and has produced much of the whisky for Bell's blends ever since. Diageo owns it today. A couple of limited edition single malts have been released.

**Visitor Centre**

No

**Address:** Buckie, Moray AB56 5AB
**Phone:** +44 1542 836700
**Web:** www.malts.com/en-gb/brands/
inchgower

# Kininvie

Founded in 1990, Kininvie is a largely experimental distillery. It occupies a site in Dufftown alongside The Balvenie, and has nine stills which it has run independently to create its own style and trial bottlings. Some have been released to market, but the bread and butter of this distillery is in producing whisky for blends for owner William Grant & Sons (you'll find it used in Clan MacGregor).

**Visitor Centre**

No

**Address:** Kininvie Works, Dufftown, Banffshire, Scotland, AB55 4BB
**Web:** www.kininvie.com

# Knockando

Named after the dark hillock, or 'Cnoc-an-Dhu', this distillery began life in the 1890s to produce whisky for blends. Since the 1960s it has been a constituent part of J&B. It has 4 stills and produces 1.8 million litres per annum, including its own single malts which are popular in Europe.

**Visitor Centre**

No

**Address:** Knockando, Moray AB38 7RT
**Phone:** +44 1479 847660
**Web:** www.malts.com/en-gb/brands/knockando

# Knockdhu

Knockdhu was named after the nearby Knock Hills (or Black Hills), where the source of water for this distillery comes from. You might not recognise its name immediately, but you probably will have heard of its famous line of single malt whiskies under the anCnoc brand.

Founded in 1893 by the recently-formed Distillers Company Limited (DCL), which went on to become Diageo, this was an early combined grain and malt distillery, producing both styles of whisky. Despite its lofty location, it was well served by railway and local elements essential for production.

Closed in 1983, Inver House bought it in 1989 and set about reviving its fortunes whilst keeping the original equipment (remaining at

only two stills) and buildings where possible.

**Visitor Centre**

Daily tours are held at 10am and 2pm, lasting up to 2 hours. You can learn about the history of Knockdhu, ask questions, speak to the production team, and sample the current range (drivers get some to take home). You must book in advance.

**Address:** Knock by Huntly, Aberdeenshire AB54 7LJ
**Phone:** +44 1466 771223
**Web:** www.ancnoc.com

# Linkwood

Built on the Linkwood House estate in 1821, this was a small, independent distillery for the early part of its life. It was expanded in the 1870s, and new buildings opened in the 1970s, and also in 2012. Diageo owns it today, producing malt for blends with a 2.5 million litre capacity, produced from 6 stills. A 12-year-old single malt has been produced under the Flora & Fauna range, as well

as some other occasional independent bottlings.

**Visitor Centre**

No

**Address:** Linkwood Road, Elgin, Moray IV30 8RD
**Phone:** +44 1343 547004
**Web:** www.malts.com/en-gb/brands/linkwood

# Longmorn

Long seen as a luxury whisky brand, Longmorn is a Speyside distillery with class and good standing. Founded by John Duff and partners in 1894, it occupies a sacred spot where a chapel once stood, and has grown into a major brand under the ownership of Chivas Brothers. The distillery today has a capacity of 4.5 million litres, and the original smooth shouldered stills designed by Duff are still in place. Their broadness gives their whisky depth, smoothness and fruitiness. The maturation process enhances this further by the use of first-fill casks. Other sherry and both American and traditional oak casks are also available to enhance the range.

Having said that, the stills were modified to make them more energy efficient in keeping with the company's ethos.

While connoisseurs croon over their products – particularly the 23-year-old which won Gold in 2017's International Wine and Spirits Competition – much of Longmorn's product goes to make blends such as Chivas Regal 18-year-old and the Royal Salute Range. Longmorn is sadly not open to the public.

**Address:** Longmorn Cres, Elgin IV30 2SJ
**Phone:** +44 1542 783042

## Visitor Centre

No

# The Macallan

The Macallan is one of the great names in Scottish single malt whisky distilling. Founded in 1824 on Easter Elchies Farm, it had a fairly quiet start and plodded along until being sold in 1892 to Roderick Kemp. His family and descendants continued running the distillery until expansion and modernisation in the 1960s and a greater focus on single malts over blends began to shape the output. The Macallan's famous 10-year-old (one of the best-selling single malts) was released in 1978. The distillery was sold to Highland Distillers in 1996, and it is here that The Macallan story really began to take off.

While its choice of finishing in sherry casks was considered unusual and part of the popular flavour of The Macallan, it began using bourbon casks in the early 2000s which resulted in a change in the flavour and range on offer.

The Macallan is now a large producer, with 12 wash and 24 spirit stills, 21 washbacks, and a

**Address:** Easter Elchies, Aberlour AB38 9RX
**Phone:** +44 1340 318000
**Web:** www.themacallan.com

## Visitor Centre

A visitor centre was opened in 2001, and in 2014 this was superseded by the present facility which is one of the best among Scotland's whisky distilleries. With stunning architecture and interiors, guests are taken on an immersive experience through the proud heritage of The Macallan. Various tours are on offer of different lengths and prices, and should be booked in advance. The Elchies Brasserie offers a gastronomic experience paired with The Macallan Distil Your World London Single Cask. You can also relax in The Macallan Bar. The Distillery Boutique sells produce, limited edition bottles and other gift items.

capacity for 15 million litres per annum. Water is sourced form boreholes on the estate.

Today's new distillery and visitor centre buildings are designed to produce electricity through a new biomass generator, which also feeds local houses. The wonderful location of the distillery in the Elchies Forest, with its wonderful views, is well worth discovering.

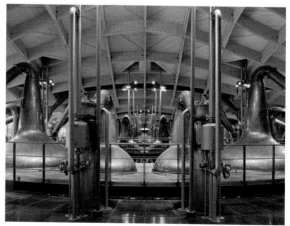

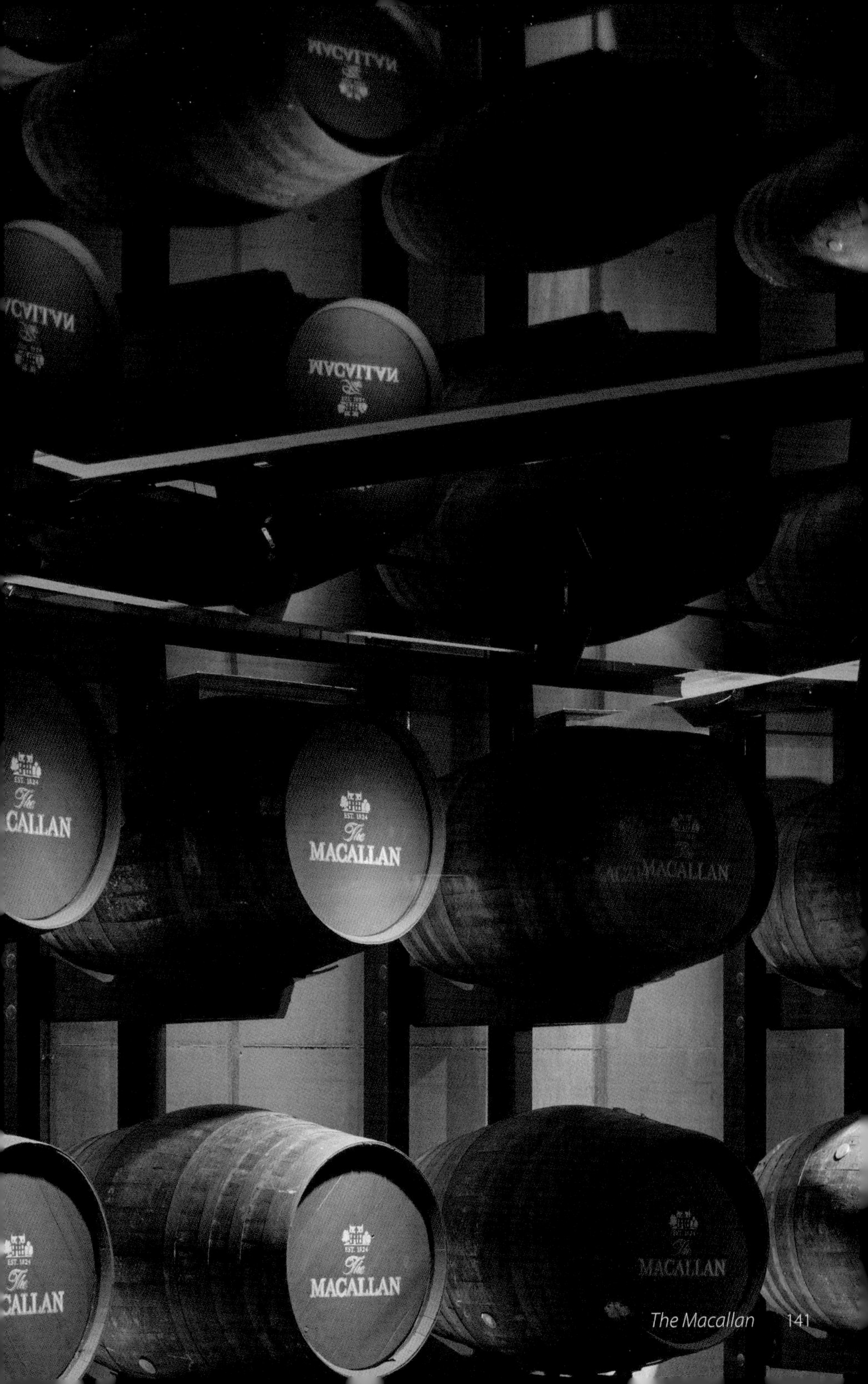
EST. 1824
The
MACALLAN

# Mannochmore

Rarely producing any of its own single malt, Mannochmore is a distillery which produces malt for blends like Haig. The distillery was opened in 1971, and its most famous own bottling was the Loch Dhu whisky, which is now out of production. Its staff are shared with nearby Glenlossie distillery. Mannochmore does not offer tours.

**Visitor Centre**

No

**Address:** Glenlossie Rd, Thomshill, Elgin IV30 8GY
**Phone:** +44 1343 862000
**Web:** www.malts.com/en-gb/brands/mannochmore/

# Miltonduff

Part of Pernod Ricard, Miltonduff in Elgin produces malt for Ballantine's Finest blend, with only its 16-year-old cask strength as its own bottling. The distillery uses two stills, and matures its produce in American oak barrels. It has an output capacity of 5,500,000 litres per year, making it one of Scotland's largest. Various limited releases have been made over the past decades, including two under Gordon & MacPhail, and one under Douglas Laing.

**Visitor Centre**

A reception centre is located at the distillery, but any tours must be arranged in advance

**Address:** Lochiepots Road, Elgin, Morayshire IV30 8TG
**Phone:** +44 1343 554121

# Mortlach

A Speyside distillery, and the first to be licensed in Dufftown, opening in 1823. After a confusing period of changes of ownership and use, the distillery began providing malt for blends such as Johnnie Walker. Then, in 1995, its first single malt was released.

Since then the Mortlach brand has grown in stature and a number of standard and special edition bottlings have been produced, even though its popularity for blends continues.

Mortlach was doubled in capacity in 2014 when a mirror image of the distillery was created next door, allowing greater freedom to produce more of its own stock. It uses six stills, with one of these acting as an intermediate to add richness, before condensing in worm tubs.

**Visitor Centre**

No

**Address:** Dufftown, Moray, AB55 4AQ
**Phone:** +44 1340 820318
**Web:** www.malts.com/en-row/brands/mortlach

# Roseisle

If you've ever wondered which is the largest Scottish whisky distillery, then Roseisle is your answer. Opened by Diageo in 2010, it covers 3,000sq m and has one of the largest outputs, at 10 million litres per annum. It incorporates a biomass facility to generate its own electricity, and recovers heat for its maltings nearby. Its malts are used in Buchanan and Johnnie Walker blended whiskies.

**Visitor Centre**

No

**Address:** Roseisle, Moray IV30 5YP
**Phone:** +44 1343 832100

# Speyburn

Set in quite a unique spot for a distillery, in a narrow glen known as the Granty Burn up near Rothes, Speyburn was established in 1897. The pure waters of the stream running through the Burn gives Speyburn its refreshing flavour, and it is the only distillery to use this water. Famously a whisky was produced here for Queen Victoria's Diamond Jubilee when the site first opened.

**Visitor Centre**

No

**Address:** Rothes, Aberlour, Banffshire AB38 7AG
**Phone:** +44 870 888 1314
**Web:** www.speyburn.com

# Speyside

One of Scotland's smallest, and oldest, distilleries, originating from the 1760s. Situated near Kingussie in Inverness-shire, it has two stills capable of producing 600,000 litres per year. The present-day distillery was revived and rebuilt stone-by-stone near the original between the 1960s and 80s. Speyside's malt whisky range comes under the SPEY branding, and comes in various ages and limited edition bottlings.

**Visitor Centre**

No

**Address:** Tromie Mills, Kingussie PH21 1NS
**Phone:** +44 1479 810126
**Web:** www.speysidedistillery.co.uk

# Strathisla

Strathisla is perhaps one of the unluckiest distilleries, but is also one of the most loved and visited.

Founded in 1786, for 165 years it was mostly known as the Milltown Distillery. Through the late 1800s the distillery suffered a fire and an explosion which badly damaged its buildings. But it soldiered on producing Strathisla whisky. It suspended operations during the First World War, and in 1950 was sold to Chivas Brothers. They decided to change its name to that of its most famous product.

**Address:** Seafield Ave, Keith AB55
**Phone:** +44 1542 783044
**Web:** www.chivas.com/en-GB/visit-strathisla

## Visitor Centre

A gift shop, museum and distillery tours are available at Strathisla. Telling the history of this old distillery as well as Chivas Brothers, it makes a good day out and more of a introduction to whisky for the uninitiated than at other distilleries.

Today the site has four stills producing nearly 2.5 million litres per annum of its own Strathisla single malts, as well as whisky for Chivas Regal blend. It sources water from Fons Bullen Well, which is free from peat and gives a smoother flavour.

As Scotand's oldest continually operated distillery, Strathisla also has some of its prettiest buildings. Lots of whisky fans and tourists visit each year to learn of its history and that of Chivas Brothers.

# Strathmill

This former corn mill was turned into a whisky distillery in the 1890s, with many original buildings still used. It was originally called Glenisla-Glenlivet until 1895. Today it is owned by Diageo and used for producing whisky for blends like J&B, with four stills and a 1.8 million litre per annum capacity. It is not open to the public.

**Visitor Centre**

No

**Address:** Keith, Moray AB55 5DQ
**Phone:** +44 1542 883000
**Web:** www.malts.com/en-row/brands/strathmill

# Tamdhu

Founded in 1896 in a wave of new Speyside distilleries, Tamdhu has survived. Its main reception centre is the old Knockando station, on a line that meant the region's whiskies could reach a wider audience.

Closed for a year in 2010, it is now producing a new 10-year-old and some special editions.

**Address:** Knockando, Aberlour AB38 7RP
**Phone:** +44 1506 852205
**Web:** www.tamdhu.com

**Visitor Centre**

Not open to the public. Limited tours are available during the Spirit of Speyside Whisky Festival.

# Tamnavulin

Tamnavulin opened in 1966 and was immediately destined for large-scale production for blenders Whyte & Mackay. They bought it in 1993, but closed Tamnavulin down two years later. It passed through various owners before resuming production again in 2007, after having an upgrade of its facilities. Today it produces its own single malt rich in Speyside character. Tamnavulin means 'mill on the hill', referring to an old mill building on the site.

**Visitor Centre**

No

**Address:** Tomnavoulin, Moray AB37 9JA
**Phone:** +44 1479 818031
**Web:** www.tamnavulinwhisky.com

# Tomintoul

Tomintoul is the highest village in the Highlands, and its own distillery nearby that has been here since 1964. It has four stills and produces a range of single malts and whisky for blends. With relatively modern buildings, it uses traditional techniques to produce both peated and unpeated whisky – the latter described as "the gentle dram". It even produced the world's biggest ever bottle of whisky in 2009, at 105.3 litres!

**Visitor Centre**
Only by appointment.

**Address:** Tomintoul, Ballindalloch AB37 9AQ
**Phone:** +44 1807 590274
**Web:** www.tomintoulwhisky.com

# Tormore

Built in 1958 to produce whisky for blends, Tormore has more recently expanded to include its own 14- and 16-year-old single malts in addition to its core business. This is a large distillery, owned by Pernod Ricard and operated by Chivas Brothers. You can hardly miss it thanks to its copper roof and tall chimney next to the main road. It was designed by leading architect Sir Albert Richardson. Its location is spectacular, on the edge of the Cairngorms National Park.

**Visitor Centre**
No

**Address:** Richardson Road, Advie, Grantown-on-Spey, Moray PH26 3LR
**Phone:** +44 1807 510244
**Web:** www.tormoredistillery.com

# Scotland's Best Whisky Bars

**VISITING DISTILLERIES IS** an important way of learning how whisky is made, getting to know the passion its creators have for their product, and trying it fresh from the cask. But unless you visit lots of distilleries, you will only be able to sample a few different whiskies.

Thankfully Scotland has many bars, both traditional and modern, dedicated to the water of life, and in this section we list some of the best known and most popular to try. Most will have an extensive selection of whiskies from all distilleries, including rare and vintage bottles to try. We recommend:

## Dornoch Castle Hotel

Voted the best whisky bar in Scotland by various outlets. Set inside the historic castle hotel (which now has a distillery in operation). It has a wide range of rare and premium malts from around the world, and is served by knowledgeable staff. Hosts the Dornoch Whisky Festival.

**Castle Street, Dornoch IV25 3SD**
**+44 1862 810216**
**www.dornochcastlehotel.com**

## Amber Whisky Bar

The bar in the basement of Edinburgh's Scottish Whisky Experience. It serves over 380 whiskies, has knowledgeable staff, and interactive touchscreens with information about distilleries. Also serves food.

**354 Castlehill, Edinburgh EH1 2NE**
**+44 131 477 8477**
**www.scotchwhiskyexperience.co.uk/**
**restaurant**

## The Quaich Bar at the Craigellachie Hotel

Set in one of the finest hotels in Scotland, and surrounded by many great distilleries. The Quaich Bar offers over 700 single malts, and great locally-sourced food in the adjoining restaurant.

**Victoria St, Craigellachie, Speyside AB38 9SR**
**+44 1340 881204**
**www.craigellachiehotel.co.uk/the-quaich/**

# Fiddler's Bar & Restaurant

A great food and drink destination. The bar has a whisky library and menu to choose from, which covers almost every Scottish whisky you can imagine. Staff offer tips, especially on pairing with your food.

**The Green Mainstreet, Drumnadrochit, Inverness IV63 6TU**
**+44 1456 450678**
**www.fiddledrum.co.uk**

# Usquabae

A whisky bar set in the haunting surroundings of the Edinburgh Vaults. Has over 400 whiskies on offer, and serves food.

**2-4 Hope Street, Edinburgh EH2 4DB**
**+44 131 290 2284**
**www.usquabae.co.uk**

# The Ardshiel Hotel

The go-to spot for drinking whisky in Campbeltown. This is a popular and historic family-run hotel dating from 1877. Hundreds of whiskies are on offer in its bar.

**Kilkerran Rd, Campbeltown PA28 6JL**
**+44 1586 552133**
**www.ardshiel.co.uk**

# The Grill

One of Aberdeen's oldest and most famous bars. Famous in our eyes for having over 600 single malts to try. You can order a flight of four whiskies to try, or ask the staff for their recommendations.

**213 Union St, Aberdeen AB11 6BA**
**+44 1224 583563**
**www.thegrillaberdeen.co.ukk**

# The Artisan Restaurant

With over 1,300 whiskies on offer, this has to be the largest selection of any bar in Scotland. The owner has trained his staff to be well versed on the topic and can recommend a dram for you. But with this many, how do you choose?

Excellent food served, too.

**249-251 Main St, Wishaw ML2 7NE**
**+44 1698 373893**
**www.artisan-restaurant.com**

# Bon Accord

A traditional pub in central Glasgow which also has over 300 whiskies to choose from. Discerning whisky drinkers choose the pub because of its selection and atmosphere.

**153 North St, Glasgow G3 7DA**
**+44 141 248 4427**
**www.bonaccordweb.co.uk**

# Ballygrant Inn

A great choice on Islay. The Ballygrant has over 400 whiskies on offer, and an intimate knowledge (and great selection) of those which come from Islay. Located close to the Port Askaig ferry terminal.

**Ballygrant, Isle of Islay PA45 7QR**
**+44 1496 840277**
**www.ballygrant-inn.com**

# Bibliography

In preparation of this book, the following sources of reference were used. They are, of course, recommended to anyone with an interest in further reading about Scottish whisky and the country's distilleries.

## Books

*Britain in a Bottle – A Visitor's Guide*. Ted Brunning & Rupert Wheeler. Bradt. 2020
*Jim Murray's Whisky Bible 2020*. Jim Murray. Dram Good Books. 2020
*Whiskies Galore – A Tour of Scotland's Island Distilleries*. Ian Buxton. Birlinn. 2017
*World Whisky – A Nation-by-Nation Guide to the Best*. Charles MacLean. Dorling Kindersley. 2016

## Websites

*Scotch Whisky*. www.scotchwhisky.com
*The Whisky Exchange*. www.thewhiskyexchange.com
*Trip Advisor*. www.tripadvisor.co.uk
*Visit Scotland*. www.visitscotland.com
*Whisky.com*. www.whisky.com
*Wikipedia*. www.wikipedia.org

# Acknowledgements

We would like to thank all of the distilleries and their staff who have kindly supported us in producing this book. Our requests for information, photographs and updates through the challenging Covid-19 period were always met with enthusiasm for what we were doing, and with natural desire for the world to know that their amazing distilleries were still open and keen to welcome people to visit again. Without their support this book would not have been possible.

# Picture Credits

# INDEX